Uncomfortable

Childhood Sexual Abuse, PTSD,
What I Wish I had Known, and
The Cost of Silence

W.J. Novack

Copyright © 2021 William J. Novack
All rights reserved. No part of this publication may be reproduced, distributed, or transmitted in any form or by any means without prior written permission from the author, except brief excerpts for review purposes.

ISBN: 9798588201360

For those of us not yet aware of the questions.

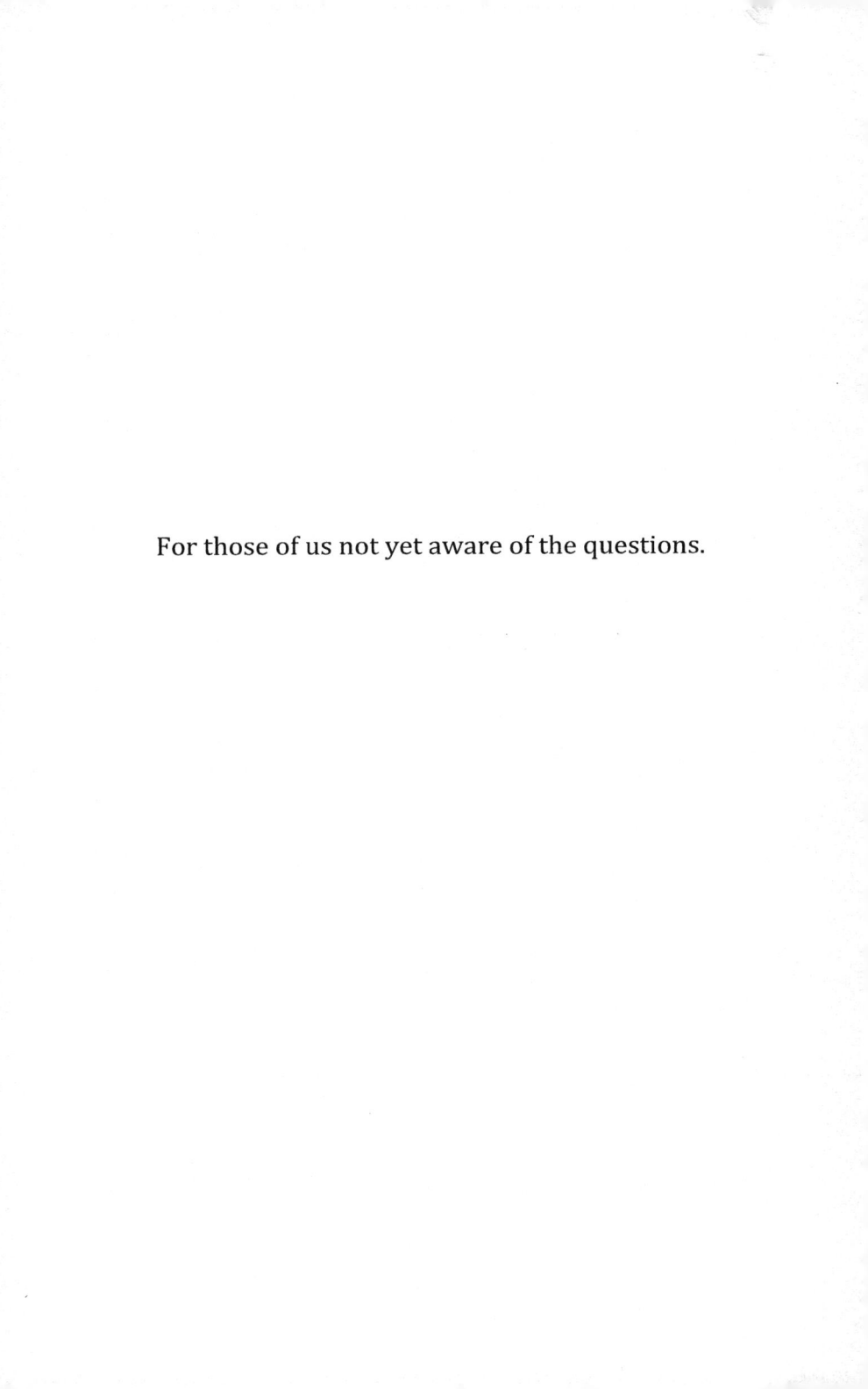

Table of Contents

Introduction	9
Chapter 1 - Uncomfortable	23
Chapter 2 - My Childhood	39
Chapter 3 - Dissociation	55
Chapter 4 - The Change	75
Chapter 5 - Hypervigilance	91
Chapter 6 - Codependancy	101
Chapter 7 - My Teenage Years	115
Chapter 8 - Adverse Childhood Experiance (ACE)	131
Chapter 9 - The Two Way Street	143
Chapter 10 - Pornography Addiction and Healing	157
Chapter 11 - Sexual Disfunction	169
Chapter 12 - Untying the Knots of Our Emotions	177
Chapter 13 - The Path Toward Healing	197
Chapter 14 - Final Thoughts	229
Author's Notes	233

Introduction

> So hold me Jesus,
> Cause I'm shaking like a leaf
> You have been King of my glory
> Won't You be my Prince of Peace
>
> —Rich Mullins, "Hold Me Jesus"

There I stood on a remote street, alone in the dark, completely naked. I was drunk out of my mind and yelling toward Heaven at the top of my lungs.

The place was not always the same, but the fact that I was intoxicated, naked, and crying out to God for help was nothing new.

I had no idea what was happening to me as I stood there shaking with broken beer bottles covering the road around my bare feet, pleading for help. "God, what the f**k is wrong with me? Why do I keep doing this?" I screamed into the night.

This was not the first time such a scene had played out in my life, but it was the last. A short time later, God reached out and grabbed me by the collar and shook until I was done. It is here that I begin this story. Only God could orchestrate the chaos that was my life into what it has become today. There is nothing clean and neat about my story. Likewise, there is nothing clean and neat about this book. I can assure you it will get downright messy at times.

In 2008 I encountered God in a way that I didn't at first recognize as being God. He radically disassembled every aspect of my life and then reassembled my world into something that I never thought possible.

Rich Mullins must have been referring to this same God that I encountered when he said, "God is a wild man . . . should you encounter Him . . . hang on for dear life—or let go for dear life is a better way to say it." I chose to let go, not knowing or caring if I would survive. I hit the end of myself so hard that I didn't care if I lived or died.

The fact that I was drunk and naked had absolutely nothing to do with sex—or did it? I should say it had nothing to do with a desire for sex. At the time I had no idea what was happening to me other than that I was unbearably uncomfortable. I had been uncomfortable for most of my life and had no real understanding of why. At the time I didn't recognize that my life had been one long, frustrating journey to find some semblance of peace, to find lasting comfort.

This is what being sexually abused as a child does to a person. Quite often it leaves victims physically wounded, but the emotional scars that it inflicts are the most damaging. For many children, sexual abuse goes undetected, and all too often if it is brought to the light, it is minimalized. We have all heard phrases like "kids are tough" or "he or she will bounce back in no time."

The harsh reality is that although many children learn to live with the aftermath of abuse, they are ticking time bombs, headed toward a debilitating self-destructive future. I have a deep desire to reach out to others who have suffered childhood trauma. Millions of souls suffer from anxiety, addictions, and physical ailments and have no idea why. Much like me, they go through life living day to day with feelings of being discontent and uncomfortable emotionally and all too often physically.

Many of us live under the pretense that the further we distance ourselves from our childhood, the better we will feel because we believe the lie that "time heals all wounds." As evidenced by the story of my life, such fables of time and healing do not hold water emotionally, psychologically, or scientifically. Many of us have learned to stuff the memories of our past so far into a dark corner somewhere that we have all but forgotten the reason for our pain, yet it continues to poison every aspect of our lives.

In the past thirty to forty years, a growing body of evidence has linked childhood sexual abuse with psychological disorders such as PTSD and physically debilitating autoimmune and nervous system disorders.

The subtitle of this book is "Childhood Sexual Abuse, PTSD, What I Wish I Had Known, and the Cost of Silence." This book is about sharing all the things that I have learned about the devastating aftereffects of childhood sexual abuse. If I had known what I have learned over the past ten years thirty years ago, it would have undoubtedly saved me years of psychological and physical suffering—not only my suffering but also the suffering I have inflicted on the world around me through my chaotic and disruptive behavior. I will discuss in detail the cost of silence that is paid by far too many of us.

Albert Einstein wrote in his highly controversial 1954 essay "Religion and Science" that "Science without religion is lame, religion without science is blind." There has long been contention between the proponents of these two points of view—the two camps being so caught up in the pride of proving their position that they have become blinded to the truth held in both science and religion.

I spent over two decades immersed in the Christian subculture. In many ways my life was enriched through that experience, but in others I was worse off after twenty years than when I started. I spent years being indoctrinated with the belief that psychology is bad and nothing more than "psychobabble"—a term that I and my fellow believers used regularly.

I was in my mid-forties before I was introduced to the term PTSD (post-traumatic stress disorder) and much of its associated jargon, as associated with child abuse. I had always associated PTSD with soldiers returning home from war, not victims of child abuse.

At age forty-three, the time bomb finally detonated, and my life came apart at the seams. The reality of my past caught up with me so hard and so fast that it disassembled every aspect of my world. The pain was inescapable. The past that I had fought my entire life to ignore and even deny had caught up with me and was not letting go.

If someone had insinuated that I was suffering from PTSD a year before my life was so abruptly derailed, I would have said they were crazy. I was on top of the world. My business was booming, and things were going as well as could be expected with my family. I was a deacon in our church. Life was just getting good, but little did I know that in the not-so-distant future, my life would be abruptly and dramatically changed.

The best way I can describe what happened is that I came undone. Twenty years ago I would have been labeled as having a nervous breakdown—a term that has since been abandoned by the mental health community. I was out of control. I began self-medicating heavily with alcohol and pornography. Sleep was unattainable and mocked me for weeks. I would sleep for twenty or thirty minutes at a time and awaken in a panic attack, gasping for air. Falling asleep became something I dreaded. As hard as I tried, I was unable to escape the realities of life and my past.

Through a series of events that I can only describe a supernatural, I landed at a church that loved me through my manic and irrational state. They referred me to a counseling center for sexually abused children. God had begun to answer the question, "What's wrong with me?", that I had screamed into the darkness just a few months earlier.

I had attended church regularly for most of my adult life but could not find the peace for which I was searching. I would go for long periods, months and even years, feeling very secure in my faith. Then at times, seemingly out of nowhere, I would become unsettled and pick up my old habits of self-medicating. It had become a continuous cycle, and the longer I stayed in church, the deeper I would retreat into my shame.

The idea of acknowledging that I was an addict or suffered from mental illness was unthinkable. I had become very good at hiding my addiction from others and lying to myself. The Christian subculture that I was involved with viewed mental illness as weakness. The church that I had been attending for over five years before I finally came to the end of myself viewed any type of illness as a lack of faith. A common phrase was "The world may say you are sick, but the truth is that you are healed by His stripes," meaning the suffering of Jesus Christ (Isaiah 53:5). Yes, Jesus can and does heal us, but we were missing part of the equation.

The good news is that along my journey I discovered a growing community of Bible-believing Christians who have embraced the discoveries of science and modern psychology. Many of these men and women are helping those within the Church understand that mental illness is a treatable disorder and not merely a lack of faith.

As we journey through these pages, we will delve into the science of psychology. Although the record shows that Einstein had a difficult time believing in a God who is involved with His Creation on a personal level, it is clear that he recognized the fingerprints of intelligent design spread across our physical universe. For me, learning about the magnificent complexities of the mind and human psychology reinforces my faith in God. I stand in awe of His Creation. I often wonder if our Father in Heaven breaks out in a coy grin, brimming pride when His children discover one of the complexities of His Creation, such as gravity, the speed of light, or the brain's limbic system. After all, what good father could resist?

In all my years of pastoral and Christian counseling, I never heard terms such a *hypervigilance, dissociation, adverse childhood experience (ACE),* or *dysautonomia*. These are all terms that I wish I had understood so many years ago. My life may have been much different. I will discuss all of these terms and many others as we move along. The science of psychology is not "psychobabble" any more than religion is "nothing more than mere superstition." God heals, but His people are perishing because of ignorance (Hosea 4:6). Much of the terminology associated with psychology may sound a bit foreboding, but let me assure you that as we continue, we will learn that such terminology is not to be feared. This language is nothing more than words given to help describe the human condition.

If you can relate to my experience with my church, I believe that as we move along you will find a roadmap that will help you begin to heal. If you are a pastor and have encountered people like me under your care, I hope you will listen to my heart as you turn the pages. I have no doubt that you have encountered many people like me. I feel confident saying this because I know there are countless others just like me seeking healing in churches all around the world.

For the minister is called to recognize the sufferings of

> *his time in his own heart and make that recognition the starting point of his service. Whether he tries to enter into a dislocated world, relate to a convulsive generation, or speak to a dying man, his service will not be perceived as authentic unless it comes from a heart wounded by the suffering about which he speaks.*[1]
>
> *—Henri Nouwen - The Wounded Healer: Ministry in Contemporary Society*

This heart that Henri Nouwen speaks of is not necessarily wounded through shared experience. Christ did not weep with Mary and Martha at Lazarus's tomb because He lacked faith as they did but out of deep compassion (John 11:35). Jesus did not enter into His Creation to understand but to suffer with those He loves. He dares to enter into the inner person and dwell with us in all of the joy and suffering of this life.

As I fought my way through recovery, I discovered something interesting. I experienced the same reluctance to accept mental illness as a legitimate cause for physical disorders from the medical community as I did with those in the Church. When I say physical illness, I am including conditions such as anxiety and depression along with autoimmune, autonomic nervous system, and many other disorders and sicknesses. Anyone who suffers with anxiety attacks and depression understands all too well that our bodies share in the experience. At the suggestion of such an idea, I would receive the same look from many of my doctors as I received from my pastor. Why the reluctance? This is a question that I will do my best to answer after I share a little more of my story.

Just as I started to feel that I was back on my feet emotionally, my journey took a new and unexpected turn. I

---

[1] Henri J. M. Nouwen, *The Wounded Healer: Ministry in Contemporary Society* (New York: Image Books, 1972), xvi.

began experiencing neurological issues that we later discovered were associated with PTSD. I have been prescribed anxiety medication many times throughout my life. I have heard people say that "stress is a killer" for years, but I had no idea that it was literally killing me. Stress had become a way of life, the atmosphere in which I lived. I hated the way anxiety medication made me feel, or should I say, "not feel." I had lived for so long with my body being marinated by stress hormones that the feeling had become normal.

In 2014 I was diagnosed with Proximal Atrial Fibrillation (AFib). I was treated with a metaphysical approach through the wonders of pharmacology. Again, I resisted the medication because I hated the way it made me feel, and it did very little or nothing to stop my AFib.

A short time later I was diagnosed with sleep apnea, which at the time was considered by my doctor to be a possible reason for my AFib. Despite a couple of years of sleeping with a BiPAP machine, and my health continued to decline.

In 2016 I began writing this book without the understanding that my health issues could possibly be associated with PTSD. A year earlier, in 2015, I published a book titled *Purgatory: Heaven's Healing Waters*. It's a book about God's healing touch in the lives of His children. I shared my history of abuse as a child and that I had come to a place of forgiveness and love toward my abusers. Several readers suggested I consider writing a book about my recovery. I wasn't sure I was ready for such an endeavor, but the idea tugged on my heartstrings. As with so much in life, God asks us to step into the unknown as He takes us by the hand. As it turns out, I wasn't ready, but God was. Little did I understand that writing this book was as much about my continued healing as sharing my experiences and what I have learned.

Soon after I began writing, I started experiencing severe anxiety attacks and depression. I was finding it impossible to sleep once again. I would sleep for short periods, only to wake, gasping for air and my heart beating out of control. At the time, my therapist asked me what I was feeling just after waking, and the best I can describe the first moments is that it was as if death had become a person and was in the room with me, glaring just inches from my face. I had become fixated on my own mortality. I was beginning to doubt if I was even close to being qualified to write about healing.

I began having heart palpations—at times several per minute. I was also diagnosed with irritable bowel syndrome and gastric reflux. For almost a year, I was unable to function without a steady diet of antacids and laxatives. I even purchased a special bed, so I could sleep with my head and chest elevated to help with the perpetual feeling of heartburn.

In 2018 I finally received a diagnosis that helped me begin to put the pieces together. At the Mayo Clinic in Jacksonville, Florida, I was diagnosed with cardiovagal failure and a low HRV (heart rate variability) score. Both conditions fall within the broader heading of dysautonomia—an all-encompassing term used to describe a myriad of symptoms associated with autonomic nervous system disruption.

Let me give an abbreviated explanation of what this diagnosis means. Many of our body's electrical impulses are regulated by what is called the ANS (autonomic nervous system). This system is made up of two interdependent subsystems called the sympathetic and the parasympathetic systems. The SNS (sympathetic nervous system) is responsible for revving up our bodies when needed—somewhat like pressing the gas pedal in a car. The PSNS (parasympathetic nervous system) is responsible for calming our bodies—throttling down and applying the brakes. Much of the function of the PSNS is controlled through the vagus nerve. The vagus nerve runs from the base of our brain and meanders, relaying signals from our brain to our organs all the way down to our lower abdomen. It connects just about everything to everything.

When we breathe in, the SNS releases a stress hormone that causes our heart rate to increase, and when we breathe out, the PSNS through the vagus nerve slows the heart. You can detect this for yourself. Find your pulse in your wrist and slowly breathe in. You will feel your pulse increase. And when you slowly breathe out, you will feel your pulse decrease. This is part of what your doctor is doing when he or she is listening to your heart with a stethoscope and asks you to breathe in and breathe out. They are listening for the way your heart responds.

When our ANS is sending proper signals to our heart via the vagus nerve, this speeding up and slowing down should vary slightly between heartbeats. When this happens it indicates that the heart is responding to signals from the autonomic nervous system. When it doesn't happen, it could because there is a communication problem between the ANS and the heart.

When I asked if this is something that would get better, the doctor said he wasn't sure. He said some people get better and some get worse. Yes, he was being vague. Unfortunately, in the culture of western medicine, conditions without a pharmacological remedy all too often go untreated. If there is no incentive for a big payoff through the sale of drugs, research money is limited.

He went on to explain that some medications can help reduce the uncomfortable feelings associated with the disorder, but the key to getting better is reducing stress, which is something I have failed at miserably for most of my life.

I had two choices at that point: 1) do nothing and spend the rest of my shortened life on disability and heavily medicated or 2) dig in and use the mind that God gave me to figure out how to get better.

I chose the latter and began reading everything I could on the subject of PTSD and neurological disorders. I quickly realized I was not alone. A few simple searches on the Internet, and I uncovered countless books and articles linking neurological and autoimmune disorders to trauma. Many of the case studies and articles that I read could have been about me.

I must admit that I was angry at first. Why such a disconnect between the undeniable mountain of evidence and our medical community? When we begin to understand that western medical schools do not teach a holistic approach to medicine, we will begin to understand the disconnect.

Western medicine is a system of specialists who treat symptoms and are trained to have very little interest in the "hows and the whys" and instead are taught to heal through pharmacology or surgery. For example, if your heart is beating out of rhythm, they understand what medications or procedures may help, but little thought, if any, is given to the body as a whole. To further illustrate the point, when I asked my cardiologist if my irritable bowel syndrome could be affecting my heart, he said he had no idea and recommended that I see a gastroenterologist. When the subject of PTSD came up, he sent me to a psychiatrist.

Please do not misunderstand what I am saying. I am very grateful for all the advancements in modern medicine. My life has been significantly improved through our medical system, but sometimes we need to connect the dots for ourselves.

Let's return to the question above: why are doctors

reluctant to accept mental illness as a legitimate reason for physical illness? The answer, to put it bluntly, is ignorance and fear. Most of us who have received any type of sales training have heard the saying, "A confused mind always says no." It is human nature to resist what we do not understand.

It stands to reason that the way we overcome this resistance and fear is through understanding (knowledge). So, the short answer is through compassion, a word that is ubiquitous in our world, though somewhat misunderstood. As we grow in knowledge, we will discover that compassion is many things, one of which is the evidence of understanding. Compassion is also proof that we are in the presence of love. The Word of God tells us that "There is no fear in love, but perfect love casts out fear." (1 John 4:18) Henri Nouwen writes, in his book *The Wounded Healer,* "For a compassionate man nothing human is alien: no joy and no sorrow, no way of living and no way of dying."[2]

It is not possible to travel the path that leads toward healing without walking in the authority of compassion.[3] As we move forward, we will learn that compassion is much more than a concept. Compassion is not only necessary for healing to begin, it is palpable and life giving and has authority over Creation.

This book is in no way intended to be an all-encompassing guide to PTSD and the healing of trauma, but is intended as a starting place. I quote many resources written by experts in the field of childhood sexual abuse, traumatic stress, and recovery. It is my hope that you will obtain and read the books and articles that I reference. I hope you will view them as trail markers as you progress along your path of healing.

---

[2] Nouwen, *The Wounded Healer,* 41.
[3] Ibid.

My greatest desire for you, dear reader, is that you will find hope in the pages that follow and an avenue for recovery for yourself or another—if nothing else, a place to begin. I am not a mental health professional, a priest, or a pastor. I'm just a guy with something to share. I will share my hurts and fears, hopes and dreams, what I have learned from my experiences and from others along the way, my ideas of God and who He has become in my life, and what I have found to be the most beneficial avenues of healing.

As you journey through the pages, you will find areas labeled as "rabbit trails." Rabbit trails are side trails that I take from time to explore bits of background, foundational, or related information that I believe readers may find interesting.

Much of what you are about to read is weighty, as are the issues involved with trauma and sexual abuse. I hope you hang in there with me as I do my best to answer all the questions that I anticipate you may have as we move along. One of the things I have learned is that there are so many important questions that we are not even aware to ask. When I began this work, I felt I had dealt with my past and was ready to move on with my life. Little did I understand that God was not through with me. I don't know that He is ever through with any of us. God is not interested in having His children just get by in life. His word so clearly communicates, "The thief comes only to steal and kill and destroy; I came that they may have life, and have it abundantly" (John 10:10). As I mentioned above, I am not so sure this endeavor is as much about God continuing His healing work in me as it is about my reaching out to others.

When God touches one of us, He touches us all. We are all in this together.

Uncomfortable

Chapter 1

Uncomfortable

> The areas in which we felt most insecure,
> unsafe, unloved, uncomfortable, embarrassed,
> angry, and generally unresolved as a child are
> the areas that we will be most prone to
> self-deception as an adult.
>
> —Cortney S. Warren,
> *Lies We Tell Ourselves:*
> *The Psychology of Self-Deception*

When I think back to the time I described at the beginning of my introduction, standing naked on a dark street and crying out to Heaven for help, I can't help but consider the account of Jesus as He encountered a man who was naked, possessed by an unclean spirit, and living in a tomb (Mark 5:1–15).

Let me begin by saying that I am not insinuating that I was possessed or inhabited by an evil spirit. What I am certain of is that I was sick in my spirit, soul, and my mind. My desire to be naked during these times had nothing whatsoever to do with sexuality in any way but rather a struggle to become comfortable. I was completely uncomfortable with who I was and my circumstances and had no idea how to change things. At the time I had neither acknowledged nor understood that the sexual and physical abuse I endured as a child was abuse, but it haunted me just the same. (I will discuss my abuse in the next chapter.)

As a child I had visited many counselors and was prescribed medication for my odd behavior. I was labeled as having a learning disability and hyperactive. This was in the 1970s, and by today's standards, I am sure I would have been diagnosed with ADHD (attention-deficit/hyperactivity disorder), a disorder attributed to the behavior of countless children who we have little idea how to deal with but who deserve so much more.

When I became a teenager, I discovered alcohol and recreational drugs. Once I started drinking, the only way I knew to stop was when the bottle was empty, I passed out, or I became violently ill. "Blacking out" was a regular occurrence. During my junior and senior years of high school, I drank before school on many days. Often I would down a half-pint of whiskey and a beer on my way to the bus stop. A 160-pound 6' 4" teenager drinking that much alcohol becomes pretty impaired. One of the things that troubles me as I think back on those days is that I was never reprimanded for drinking at school.

I attended a small high school in Westbrook, Connecticut, with a graduating class (1984) of around 50 students. When I consider some of the bizarre behavior displayed by the teaching staff, I often wonder what goes on in some of our country's larger schools. The reason I am sharing this and many of the issues detailed in this book are not for the purpose of telling stories about people but so you will understand that you are not alone in navigating the minefield we call childhood. I witnessed teachers with absolutely no integrity and questionable morals, not so discreetly pursuing relationships with students, selling drugs, and turning a blind eye to behavior that should have been stopped.

Marijuana and alcohol were the main drugs of choice in the social circles in which I associated. At times speed was available, and kids would also experiment with Quaaludes and acid. I remember sitting in class and being aware of my classmates coming into the room reeking of pot and so stoned that they could do little more than laugh at the teacher while making their way to their desks as they were being reprimanded for being late to class. I guess the message was that drinking and smoking weed was perfectly acceptable, but students had better not show up late for class.

Once I graduated from high school, I had no idea what I wanted to do with my life. I drank way too much, had a few odd jobs, and became engaged to be married within a couple of years after graduating. I quit drinking for a while once I was engaged, but eventually, as would be the cycle for much of my life, I went back.

In 1986 I was in debt to my father, borrowing money to start a commercial oyster fishing business. When it became apparent that things were not going well, my mother and father made me an offer that changed my life. They agreed to absolve my debt if I would join the military. At first I resisted the idea, but after experiencing a few more setbacks I decided I would "Aim High" and enlisted in the United States Air Force.

After signing my life away at the recruiter's office, I had six months until I had to show up for boot camp, which gave me time to get into plenty of trouble. Soon after my enlistment, I started drinking again, and my fiancé and I went our separate ways. About a month before I was to report for duty, I was arrested for burglary. I broke into a summer cottage looking for alcohol, but to my surprise, not being as clever as I thought myself to be, the cottage was wired with a silent alarm.

To make a long story short, once they removed the K-9 officer from my arm, I was hauled off to jail. I will never forget my father coming into the jail and looking at me through the bars and asking me if I was OK. When I told him I was, he said he would see me on Monday for my arraignment, and then he turned and walked out of the police station. I was arrested on a Thursday night, and for some reason, the courts were closed on Friday, which made for a very long weekend, giving me plenty of time to think. My parents told me several years later that those three nights that I was in jail afforded them some much-needed sleep because for once they knew exactly where I was.

Monday finally came, and I was hauled off to court and placed in a holding cell while waiting for arraignment with all of the other delinquents who had gotten into trouble over the weekend. The next hour or so in that cell was, to say the least, an eye-opener. I sat on one of the benches, and in a short time, the door was unlocked and in walked a kid I knew from high school. He was a year my junior, which meant he had been out of high school for about a year. He had been arrested for drunken disorderly conduct. He told me that he had just gotten out from a six-month "visit" at the county jail and that he was concerned because his first offense was similar to the charges he now faced.

Soon the cell began to fill, and as the stories of drunken revelry began to flow like water, it became evident that most of the fifteen or twenty men who I shared that cell with were there because of drunken acts of stupidity. Many of these guys were not much older than me and were looking at doing some real time. Many of them seemed to know one another and exchanged stories about which of their friends were in which correctional facility. It was like "Old Home Week." In that moment I realized I would do whatever it took *not* to be part of that culture.

In a couple of hours, we were led to the courtroom in

leg irons and handcuffs. My father was in the room, and let me assure you, I was humiliated. I never thought of myself as the type of person who would ever need to be in leg irons or handcuffs. I guess I had proven to the courts of Middlesex County, Connecticut, that I was.

I was arraigned and released on my own recognizance, a court date was set, and I rode home with my father. About a week after my arraignment, I received a phone call from the police department in the town in which I was arrested. They said the owner of the cottage that I had broken into would like to meet with me. I reluctantly agreed, and we met that afternoon.

Soon after entering the police station, I found myself sitting across from a Catholic priest, collar, and all. At that time I knew nothing about the Catholic Church. I am not sure I had ever even spoken to a priest before, but it made my crime feel even worse. Even being filled with foolish teenage arrogance, I knew that stealing from a priest was bad. Putting all levity aside, I know that stealing from a priest is no more wrong than stealing from anyone else, but most would agree that it carries a certain taboo.

The priest had learned that I was enrolled in the delayed enlistment program and understood that my being convicted of burglary would be the end of my chances of entering the military. Out of the kindness of his heart, and indicative of his vocation, he forgave me and said he would drop the charges if I would follow through with my enlistment and write him a letter once a month during my time in the Air Force.

I followed through with my enlistment and served my full term, going on to receive an honorable discharge, but I am not proud of the fact that I never wrote the priest a single letter. Having dyslexia and being one of the worst spellers on the face of the planet, the thought of writing even a short note scared me to death—never mind writing a letter. I have often thought of looking up the priest to apologize and thank him for his kindness. He was, as I perceived at the time, close to seventy, and that being over thirty years ago, it is likely that I will not have the opportunity on this side of Heaven.

I am confident that the priest would be happy to know that I did eventually receive Christ. I often think about the effect of this man's act of kindness and obedience to the gospel in my life. We should never underestimate the efficacy of our acts of love and kindness in obedience to the love of Christ upon those around us. We may never see the fruit of the love that we sow upon the hurting of this world, but be assured that the Lord of the Harvest is able to complete what He has begun in us (1 Corinthians 3:7–9).

On March 26, 1986, I was sworn in as an active duty member of the United States Air Force. During processing, we were required to fill out reams of paperwork. Included in that paperwork were questionnaires geared toward establishing the state of each recruit's mental health. I was honest with the questions concerning certain details of my life, which included inquiries as to how much alcohol I was accustomed to consuming.

Shortly after arriving at basic training in San Antonio, Texas, I was scheduled for regular visits with a mental health professional. Apparently, the USAF disagreed with my assessment of what was a healthy level of alcohol consumption.

I continued to receive mental health counseling throughout all four years of my enlistment. Once I completed technical school at Sheppard Air Force Base, I finished the remainder of my active duty service at Columbus Air Force Base Hospital in Columbus, Mississippi, where I worked as a medical service specialist.

My mental health doctor at Columbus Air Force Base

determined that I suffered from anxiety and felt that I should be on medication. I hated being on medication. I didn't feel like myself, which in some ways was not a bad thing. I guess I never knew what it was like to wake up and not feel like something was wrong. Anxiety and depression are conditions that I have wrestled with since childhood. I have been on and off many medications for much of my life. Some have worked well for a period, but over the long term, they have all made me feel even more depressed.

While I was home during leave between technical school and when I needed to arrive at Columbus Air Force Base, my permanent duty station, I began dating my soon-to-be wife, Mary. I say "began dating" instead of "met" because I had known Mary for quite some time. My sister had babysat her two daughters, Annie and Karan, for several years. I had pictures that Annie and Karen had drawn for me hanging on my bedroom wall throughout high school.

I had been physically attracted to Mary from the first time we met, but I was in high school, and she was eight years older than me. Neither of us thought we would ever date, never mind get married. My parents had a picnic to celebrate my coming home for leave after I finished technical school, and Mary was invited. The age difference no longer being a deterrent, one thing led to another and soon Mary became much more than the "cute chick" for whom my sister babysat.

We were married a month later, on August 30, 1986. Many of our friends and family were convinced we were crazy for getting married after only a month of dating. For the first couple of years, we did an excellent job convincing everyone that they were right. To say we fought like Titans is putting it mildly. We wanted to be together, and the only way to accomplish that was to be married. Certain financial benefits provided by Uncle Sam also made it possible for Mary and girls to move to Mississippi once we wed.

When Mary and I began our whirlwind courtship, we were both drinking heavily, and the romance was great. Relationships built on alcohol and physical romance will typically have major problems in the long term unless they undergo significant renovation.

I know we loved each other at the time, but it was only God's hand that kept us together. A month after we were married, we became pregnant. The truth of the matter was, Mary became pregnant, and I became more of a drunk. Once we received the news that we were going to have a child, Mary quit smoking and drinking immediately. We were both ecstatic about having a child. I had always wanted a family, but I was in no way prepared for things moving along so quickly. Six months earlier I wasn't even responsible for myself. Now I was government property, married, and I had children: Annie, age seven; Karen, age five; and our son, Joseph, on the way.

Mary was not only married to a drunk, she was married to a drunk while pregnant and caring for two children. One of the things that you learn when you quit drinking is that it is no fun being around someone who is drunk.

I was wondering where my fun-loving wife went. My drinking partner was gone, and the romance wasn't so good. Who wants to cozy up to a drunk who smells like stale beer and cigarettes? My poor wife sobered up, found out she was pregnant, married to a drunken moron, and living in a rundown trailer park 1,300 miles from her family and friends. I'm sure she felt like she had been left in the woods for dead. Worse than waking up from a nightmare is waking up in a nightmare from which you can't escape.

At times we may look around and wonder where God is in the chaos, but those who love Him must endeavor to remember, as impossible as it may seem at times, that God has His fingers on all the moving parts of our lives. God does not orchestrate the evil and bad things that happen throughout our lives, but He is able to take those situations, even our self-destructive behavior or the enemy's plans, and turn them into something for our good (Romans 8:28).

I will never forget when I accepted Jesus. It was in a dark, empty field in Columbus, Mississippi. I cried out to the Lord, and He answered me in the most amazing way. I knelt before Him and wept as He cracked my heart open and took me captive.

I have often heard people say that they found Christ. I can't say this was true of me. First, let me say that, as crazy as it might sound with all the horrific things that I have experienced, it is truly incredible as I look back at the book of my life that I can see God's fingerprints all over the pages, with little notes in the margins that say, "Son I love you. We are going to get through this."

I have vague memories of going to church as a child. I even have memories of reading the Bible. As with much of my childhood, I remember very little—just bits and pieces. When it was time for me to surrender to Christ as Lord of my life, I certainly didn't find Jesus. He hunted me down relentlessly.

A short time after arriving at Columbus Air Force Base, I met one of the most annoying people on the planet—I say this in love. His name was Todd Gray, and he was a Christian, and anyone within ten feet of Todd knew he was a Christian because there was no escaping him telling you about Jesus. Todd was a different type of Christian than I grew up around.

My opinion of Christians was very low at that point.

To say I had a great disdain for Christians is to put it mildly. My attitude was close to hate. I equated Christians with the Catholic kids who lived in the small town where I grew up. My family attended a few different Protestant churches when I was younger, but my experience with the Catholic kids outweighed any positive memories of going to church with my folks. My attitude about Catholics was not negative because they were overly evangelistic. On the contrary, I don't remember ever hearing anything about Jesus from a Catholic growing up. What I do remember is being bullied by wealthy snobs who could afford the best drugs and looked down at the rest of society. I realize my experience isn't representative of all Catholics at the time. I have fond memories of many Catholics, but the treatment that I received from those who were not so nice definitely tipped the scale.

The Catholics who I grew up around weren't annoying like Todd. Todd was annoying in a completely different way. Todd talked about Jesus constantly. He didn't look down at me because I wasn't rich, he didn't take the best drugs, and he didn't taunt me with the threat of physical harm because I wasn't like him. Todd was too nice. We lived in the same trailer park just off base, and he and his wife would stop by our home. Mary and I would be pretty close to rude, but they kept coming by, time and again, to tell us about Jesus.

I felt uncomfortable around Todd because he was very open about the fact that he didn't approve of drinking or the music I liked. He never came right out and said he felt that I was a sinner because I liked rock music and drank beer; it came out in his testimony. He would tell us how the Lord freed him from drinking and listening to reggae music.

Todd and his wife would explain to us how Jesus freed them from the evils of the world. They would quote Scripture, and Mary and I would ask questions, typically out of a defensive or antagonistic posture. Todd and his wife (forgive me; I don't remember her name) would just smile at our, at times, downright rude questions and keep on answering and sharing Christ's love.

Mary grew up Catholic and spent the majority of her childhood going to the same private schools as the snobby kids in my neighborhood. She had a fairly good knowledge of the Bible, but to me, what they were telling us was new. Though I was unaware of it at the time, Todd and his wife were planting seeds within my heart that would soon germinate into new life. As I thought about what they said, much of it started making sense.

At that time I had taken a part time-job selling vacuum cleaners door to door. I was very good at door-to-door sales, and soon I was selling as much as the full-time salespeople. I had no issue with telling people anything, true or not, to get them to purchase what I was selling. However, a problem began to develop when the seeds that Todd planted in my heart began to sprout.

Part of the strategy that I had developed for selling vacuum cleaners was to drive an hour or more away from Columbus to small rural neighborhoods where sales resistance was much lower. Living deep within the Bible Belt, there was no shortage of Christian radio stations, so I began to secretly tune in to Christian radio on my way to and from sales calls. I say "secretly" because the last thing I wanted was for Mary to know I was having even the slightest thought about God. However, the seeds that Todd had planted began to grow into a hunger to learn more.

Southern Baptists were one of my biggest problems during my short career as a vacuum cleaner salesman. Working in rural Mississippi, they were around every corner and under every rock. Whenever I managed to make my way into a Southern Baptist's home for a sales presentation, within five minutes of my visit, I would be hit directly between the eyes with the big question "Where do you go to church?" My standard answer was that my wife and I were looking for a church. I would follow up by declaring that I lived my life in such a way that I wouldn't do anything that I would not do in front of my wife or God. As you may have guessed, it didn't take long before I realized I needed to take another approach.

During one of our sales meetings, I asked my sales manager if he had any suggestions on how to get around the question. He told me that the answer was simple. "Tell them you attend the Methodist Church in Columbus." He reasoned that I typically worked far enough out of town that it would be highly unlikely that a Southern Baptist living in the outlying communities would be acquainted with a Methodist from Columbus. Also, he said most Southern Baptists would accept Methodism as a valid denomination and wouldn't feel the need to go any further trying to witness to me.

My sales manager hit the nail on the head, and that was the end of my problems with selling to Southern Baptists. That is, until I knocked on the door of Dr. and Mrs. McGowan from Amory, Mississippi. I don't recall exactly which denomination the McGowan's associated with, but Mrs. McGowan saw right through my line of crap. She and her husband were retired from working as dental missionaries in underdeveloped countries. They were two of the sweetest people I have ever met, but Mrs. McGowan was a pit bull (a very sweet one) for the Lord. She was on fire and was obviously on the inside track with the Holy Spirit because she didn't buy my Methodist story for one moment.

She and Dr. McGowan sat and listened to my sales pitch and even purchased one of my vacuum cleaners. We had a great time during the presentation, filled out all of the paperwork, and then she hit me with both barrels. "We have listened to you politely for the last two hours," she said. "Now you're going to sit and listen to me."

Holy crap! I felt like the proverbial whore in church. It was as if she had shot me with truth serum. She called my bluff about being a Christian, and I confessed to my deception. I sat there for what must have been well over an hour as she went to work, one hand holding an open Bible and other proclaiming the gospel with her lips. All the while Dr. McGowan sat listening with a grin from ear to ear. I often wonder if part of him might have been thinking, *I bet that poor bastard wishes he never knocked on our door.* I doubt it, but thinking back, it was evident that they both loved the Lord deeply. In all reality, he was probably praying for me and filled with the joy of the Lord.

Between Todd Gray and Mrs. McGowan, I was a mess. I didn't leave the McGowans' a believer that first day, but within a week I purchased a Bible and hid it under the seat of my car. It was one of those white gift Bibles bound with fake leather and zipped up around the edges. I hid it under my seat because I did not want Mary to know I had it.

For quite some time, I visited the McGowans' fairly regularly. I felt like I had another grandmother. Mrs. McGowan would answer any questions I had. I also went to their house just because I liked being around them. Mrs. McGowan was always very firm with me concerning spiritual matters, but she was real, and for some reason, it didn't bother me. I could tell that she genuinely cared about me. For her, sharing the Gospel was about way more than putting another notch in her belt, as was the vibe that I got with so many other Christians. Dr. McGowan never said much, but he always made me feel welcome.

After a couple of months, I finally came out of the closet with Mary concerning my Bible reading. One night Mary had gone to bed early, and I was sitting on our couch drinking a few beers and reading my Bible. Then it happened. God reached through the veil of Heaven and grabbed my heart. I walked out our back door and about a hundred yards out into the field behind our house, kneeled in the dark, and came completely undone. I was shaking uncontrollably and sobbing before the Lord, who I felt was standing directly in front of me. I have no doubt that He was and that He has been by my side ever since. I walked back into our home a changed person, never to be the same again.

After receiving Christ I spent years in confusion—lost in the shame of my childhood that I kept hidden deep within the interior recesses of my consciousness. Years of sexual, physical, and mental abuse stuffed away for no one to see or discover. I understood that I was loved, but I still carried the shame of a dark and humiliating past. The human mind is powerful and capable of things that are way beyond our understanding. Our minds can become conditioned to associate certain emotions that do not belong together, such as love and shame.

I was living in a tomb of my own making, crying out to God, while at the same time bruising myself with the stones of my past. Nobody was able to bind me—not all the pastors and counselors I had sought. I couldn't worship hard enough or read the Bible enough. Yes, perhaps I did have an unclean spirit. I can't think of how many times, just like the naked man who Jesus encountered living in the tomb, I cried out to God, "What do you have to do with me?" I did not want Him uncovering the shame of my past. I was deeply and passionately in love with Him, but there were places in my heart that I didn't want anyone to touch. And yes, that included God (Mark 5:1–15).

Satan, the enemy of my soul, had me on the ropes, screaming in my ears, "If anyone ever finds out what you've done in your past, your life is over. Do you really think that your family and friends—never mind the people you go to church with—will ever understand the things that go through your mind?"

I spent eighteen years living a "Christian life" on the outside while hiding a world of guilt, shame, and addiction. Life had become an endless field of landmines, never knowing when I would step on one and become wounded by the shame of my past.

Chapter 2

My Childhood and Abuse

> You can recognize survivors of abuse by their courage. When silence is so very inviting, they step forward and share their truth so others know they aren't alone.
>
> — Jeanne McElvaney,
> *Healing Insights:*
> *Effects of Abuse for Adults Abused as Children*

It is not uncommon for those who have suffered sexual abuse to have no memory of the event. This is the mind's way of protecting us from the memory of trauma. I have blocked out the memory of much of my childhood, which is very much a part of PTSD (post-traumatic stress disorder). All of my childhood memories before the age of about ten or twelve exist as little sound bites or short segments of video that visit my consciousness from time to time. My mother and sister often crack jokes about my not having any memories of certain events or things that most would recall—friends, family trips, and certain details of our childhood home. This does not necessarily mean my brain is blocking out multiple occurrences of sexual abuse, although I have wondered. Once the mind learns to block out the memories of a traumatic event, this tactic can become an automatic response to uncomfortable events that others would not so easily forget.

When I was a child, I was labeled as having a learning disability, suffered from dyslexia, and was considered hyperactive. By today's standards, I would have been labeled as having ADHD. (attention-deficit/hyperactivity disorder).

I also deal with what I have heard referred to as, "checking out." When exposed to a traumatic event that is more than the mind can handle, it will shut down. I have heard of this condition described as the mind pulling away within itself. In the world of psychology, this is often referred to as "depersonalization," one of the many manifestations of "dissociation."

Dissociation is a term used by mental health professionals to describe a process in which the mind learns to cope with or block out certain traumatic memories or stressful situations, like the horrors of war or being sexually molested as a child. These dissociative episodes can be as minor as daydreaming, watching a movie, and having no idea of what happened for a period of time—i.e., "checking out"—or they can be as severe as what is referred to as dissociative identity disorder (DID). We will get into dissociation in much greater detail in the next chapter.

This was part of my issue in school. My mind had learned to shut down when things got uncomfortable. In the 1993 film *The Man Without A Face*, Mel Gibson plays Justin McCloud, a man who has banished himself to a reclusive life after being disfigured in a car crash. As the story develops, it is revealed that a young boy died in the accident. To add to the plot, it is speculated that McCloud may have behaved inappropriately toward the boy. Charles "Chuck" Norstadt, played by Nick Stahl, is a young boy who suffers from an abusive past. McCloud takes Norstadt under his wing and mentors him, so he can pass a military academy's entrance exam and helps him deal with his emotional trauma. There are several scenes where Norstadt is depicted as "checking out" and staring out into space for hours at a time as a result of being confronted with the memories of his traumatic past.

Even before the movie was over, Mary started calling me Norstadt. That's because she would often walk into a room and find me sitting on a chair or on the edge of our bed, and I was gone, just staring into space for who knows how long. It would typically take some type of physical stimuli to bring me back to earth. This was long before I was diagnosed with PTSD. It still happens to this day, though not as often.

During my recovery process and my research for this book, I read countless stories of abuse and trauma as well as the litany of terminology and definitions used by mental health professionals, such as PTSD, hypervigilance, dissociation, and adverse childhood experiences (ACE). These are all terms that we will discuss as we move through this book. These terms do not define who we are. They are simply tools to help us identify and understand some of the life experiences that we encounter. For example, it has been a great comfort to realize that my not remembering much of my childhood, "checking out," or my seemingly never-ending bouts with absent-mindedness are not because I am damaged or broken. These are coping mechanisms, all under the umbrella of disassociation, experienced by many people who have dealt with trauma. Although the details of our personal stories are often different from the stories we read about in books, we can still relate to such stories emotionally.

Likewise, our personal experiences often do not fit exactly within the guidelines and definitions found in the pages of many of the books we read, and that's okay; we all experience things a little differently. At times things can get a bit confusing, especially as we attempt to assemble the puzzle of our lives. We may ask ourselves questions like, "Was what I experienced actually abuse?" or "Am I actually experiencing dissociation?" because our experiences do not fit precisely within the guidelines or examples of what we are reading. This is why it is important to seek the help of a mental health professional who specializes in abuse and PTSD. Books are not relational and are often limited by their very nature.

I want to begin this part of my story by jumping forward some forty years. When I was going through abuse counseling at the age of forty-three, my counselor gave me a book called *Abused Boys* by Mic Hunter.[1] This book has been an integral part of my healing process, and I would recommend it to anyone dealing with a sexually abusive past. However, I strongly advise doing so while seeing an abuse counselor. Some of the emotional responses that I experienced while reading *Abused Boys* were very confusing and unexpected, and it was important to have someone to talk with once those emotions began to surface.

I am not trying to frighten you away from confronting your past. Abuse counseling can be very uncomfortable, and I needed to deal with it in small doses. I would often take a break for a week or two because I needed time to breathe. Seeking an abuse counselor is one of the best decisions I have ever made. I do not think it overly dramatic to say that going through abuse counseling gave me back my life, or better said, gave me the life I never had. God heals us all in different ways and with the help of different types of people. Some of the instruments of His healing are abuse counselors.

It was while reading *Abused Boys* that I realized my

---

[1] Mic Hunter, *Abused Boys: The Neglected Victims of Sexual Abuse* (New York: Ballantine, 1990).

behavior displayed evidence of being abused long before I had any memories of being abused. The book is broken into two main sections. The first half deals with abuse from a clinical perspective. The author discusses the different emotional aspects of abuse, such as guilt, shame, and fear. He also identifies various types of abuse, helping the reader understand and recognize sexual abuse and how to identify as a victim.

The first half of the book helped me recognize and solidify the fact that I am a victim, but the second half is what really helped me understand that my behavior as a child was caused by much more than a learning disability or ADHD. This section is broken into what the author labels "Survival Stories." These are real stories by abuse survivors, written in great detail, several of which I could identify with. It was like reading my own mail. It was mind-staggering. As I read people's childhood histories and detailed accounts of their emotions, I realized I could have written the same things. When I cried out to God so many times, "What is wrong with me?", I knew this was His answer.

Now that I had the answer, what was I supposed to do with it? I spent a considerable amount of time coming to grips with the fact that something was lurking in my past that I was unable to identify. My counselor and I discussed several ways in which we could proceed, one of which was to confront my mother and father, but I quickly threw that off the table. The thought of discussing this subject with them absolutely unnerved me. I shuddered at the idea.

God has a way of working out the things that we view as impossible. One day I was driving with my mother in the car. I don't remember what we were talking about, but the conversation led to a perfect opportunity to ask her about my past. I took the chance and began by explaining what I had learned by reading *Abused Boys*. I saw the color of her face change when I asked her what happened. At first, she acted as if she had no idea what I was talking about. I continued to press her for an answer, explaining that there was nothing that she could say that would convince me that nothing happened. She finally came out with it. She and my father had gone away for a weekend when I was a toddler and left me with my uncle. I do not have all the details, nor do I need them. What I was told is that when my parents returned home, it was obvious that something was wrong. I never pushed for further explanation. I will never forget my mother's emotional state when she told me. Her eyes carried the pain of the incident as if it had happened the just day before.

Once my mother told me about the incident, I spent the next several months with this deep feeling that my entire history as a child was based on a lie and that who I thought I was, was not real. This may sound a little dramatic, but let me assure you, I was not ready for the roller coaster of emotions. I was left reaching frantically for a way of coping with my past. All the years of consoling and special classes, believing there was something wrong with me, all because I had been left alone for the weekend with my uncle. Forty-three years of believing I was born with a learning disability, dyslexia, and labeled as hyperactive to find out, that in truth, I was suffering from post-traumatic stress disorder.

I have no memory of the incident with my uncle. My counselor and I discussed the possibility of using hypnosis to unlock some of the memories of this event as well as other memories that I could be suppressing from my childhood. She didn't see the need to dig that deep, and I was in full agreement. For me, it was enough to know the reason for my behavior. I was carrying the scars of my past, and it was time to heal.

It is important for abuse victims to become survivors by discovering and acknowledging the truth without going on a crusade to discover every detail. The key to becoming a survivor is learning to put aside the shame and go through the process of understanding and truly believing that what happened is not your fault. As hard as it may be to understand in the midst of our agonizing pain, forgiveness is paramount to your survival. Trust me; I was very angry, disillusioned, and above all, hurt beyond what words can express for a long time. Once I uncovered the truth, I had every right to be angry, but there is a season for everything.

I will discuss my recovery process as we move along, but for now, it is time to continue with the story of my childhood. I know full well that I am not alone in my story. I am aware that countless others can tell a similar tale. My story is the personification of much of our culture.

I was born in 1965 in the midst of an era that has been termed the "Sexual Revolution." Hundreds of thousands of our country's young people were flocking to events like the "Summer of Love"[2] and Woodstock.[3] They had bought the lie that love is free, throwing out the social conventions of a Christian society that they felt were oppressive, such as faithfulness in marriage and purity. Pornography became an epidemic, even being touted by mainstream media as somehow good. We tapped our toes along with

---

[2] In the summer of 1967, somewhere in the neighborhood of seventy to one hundred thousand people gathered in the Haight-Ashbury neighborhood of San Francisco, California. The gathering was dubbed the "Summer of Love." For the most part, it was attended by young people who are often referred to as "hippies," or "flower children." They gathered for different reasons, including to promote the "free love" and peace movements and to protest the Vietnam War.

[3] Woodstock was a music festival held in August of 1969 at Max Yasgur's dairy farm in Bethel, New York. Half a million young adults converged in a hayfield there for what was advertised as "three days of peace and music." Drugs and alcohol flowed freely as young men and women walked naked through the crowds, uninhibited and unashamed. They kept to their agenda. It was the largest gathering of its kind in history, and there was not a single reported incident of violence.

musicians like Stephen Stills singing lyrics such as "If you're not with the one you love, love the one you're with."[4]

As a child, I remember pornography being everywhere. *Playboy* magazine was openly displayed on the coffee tables in many of my friend's homes, and if it wasn't, it could typically be found next to their fathers' beds. I remember visiting a friend of my mother who showed her the latest pornographic items that she had purchased for her husband: calendars, magazines, and a beer stein complete with a naked woman.

We grew up believing that sex was the end game. That was what it meant to become a big boy or a big girl. My mother's friend had a daughter. When we visited, we typically wanted to slip off to be alone, so we could kiss and play touchy-feely. She wasn't by any means the exception to the rule, and I was happy to play along. Sexual curiosity hung in the air like an enchantment. We were middle-school kids and younger when this was happening. We took our clothes off in front of each other, touched each other's genitals, and experimented with oral sex. Male or female, it didn't matter. We did what we saw in magazines and heard adults discussing. We thought we were "cool."

We didn't think of experimenting with sex any differently that sneaking off into the woods to smoke a cigarette that one of our friends had slipped out of their parents' packs. Here is the thing though: we always snuck off to do these things. We never did them in someone's front yard or living room. We knew they were wrong, and so did our parent's, but it didn't stop.

My parents loved me very much, but to be candid, I was more than a handful. Having little memory of my

---

[4] Stephen Stills, *Love The One You're With,* 1970, track 1 on *Stephen Stills,* Atlantic, 1970, LP.

childhood, some of what I am writing comes from stories I have heard from my family. I was the first one awake in the morning and kept pretty busy for most of the day. My mother tells me that I hated waiting to go and see if my friends could play because most of them did not wake up before daybreak. I guess in this way nothing has changed because the sun is just starting to show its face as I am writing this.

It was when I started going to school that the real issues with my behavior surfaced. I was unable to concentrate, I was hyperactive, and I had anger issues. Before I reached junior high, I was sent home from school and suspended on a couple of occasions for striking teachers. My parents had no idea how to deal with me, and they were not alone. The school system had no idea how to deal with me either.

My mom and dad were good parents, regardless of some of their faults and some of the mistakes they made along the way. They weren't perfect by any means, and they had their own issues, but I think they did a great job considering the challenges they faced. They were both very involved with my sister and me, and they got us involved in extracurricular activities. For example, they encouraged us to become active in scouting, and we were both troop leaders. I also remember my dad consistently being at my Little League and basketball games.

My sister and I grew up with one or both of our parents being at home pretty much all the time until we were in high school when my mother started to work part-time. This just proves that no matter how protective we are of our children, "crazy shit" can still happen. Many people stereotype those who become victims of sexual abuse as being from severely dysfunctional families. Sure, we had our share of dysfunction, but taking an honest look back at things, we had it pretty good. The thought of trying to raise a child like me would challenge the most qualified parent—if such a person exists.

Sometime during second grade, it was determined that I had a learning disability. For many years afterward, I was angry at this assessment, feeling it was an insult to my intelligence, but the truth is, it had nothing to do with how smart I was. I did have a problem with learning in an average classroom setting. Unknown at the time, my ability to concentrate and to deal with the stresses involved with learning in a large classroom was greatly hindered by the coping mechanism (dissociation) that my mind had developed to deal with trauma. As Donna Jackson Nakazawa states in her book, *Childhood Disrupted: How Your Biography becomes Your Biology, and How You Can Heal*,

> Those with Adverse Childhood Experiences are thirty times more likely to have behavior or learning problems than those not exposed to childhood adversity. Teachers may suggest that these children be treated for ADHD, not knowing that they need treatment for trauma or PTSD, which involves psychotherapy. The symptoms are the same, but the treatments are entirely different."[5]

The following is from a July 7, 2014, article in *The Atlantic* titled "How Childhood Trauma Could Be Mistaken for ADHD," written by Rebecca Ruiz:

> Brown was completing her residency at Johns Hopkins Hospital in Baltimore, when she realized that many of her low-income patients had been diagnosed with attention deficit/hyperactivity disorder (ADHD).

---

[5] Donna Jackson Nakazawa, *Childhood Disrupted: How Your Biography Becomes Your Biology, and How You Can Heal* (New York: Atria, 2015), 131.

> These children lived in households and neighborhoods where violence and relentless stress prevailed. Their parents found them hard to manage and teachers described them as disruptive or inattentive. Brown knew these behaviors as classic symptoms of ADHD, a brain disorder characterized by impulsivity, hyperactivity, and an inability to focus.
>
> When Brown looked closely, though, she saw something else: trauma. **Hyper-vigilance and dissociation**, for example, could be mistaken for inattention. Impulsivity might be brought on by a stress response in overdrive.
>
> 'Despite our best efforts in referring them to behavioral therapy and starting them on stimulants, it was hard to get the symptoms under control," she said of treating her patients according to guidelines for ADHD. "I began hypothesizing that perhaps a lot of what we were seeing was more externalizing behavior as a result of family dysfunction or other traumatic experience."[6]

A bit later in the article she says:

> It's not clear how many children are misdiagnosed with ADHD annually, but a study published in 2010 estimated the number could be nearly 1 million. That research compared the diagnosis rate amongst 12,000 of the youngest and oldest children in a kindergarten sample and found that the less mature students were

---

[6] Rebecca Ruiz, "How Childhood Trauma Could Be Mistaken for ADHD," *The Atlantic*, July 4, 2014, https://www.theatlantic.com/health/archive/2014/07/how-childhood-trauma-could-be-mistaken-for-adhd/373328/.

60 percent more likely to receive an ADHD diagnosis.

It was decided that it would be best if I were placed in a smaller class taught by teachers trained to deal with children with learning and behavioral challenges. This may have been a good approach, but the placement of the classroom was not very well thought out. It was situated at East Hampton, Connecticut's junior high school. Not only was it situated there, it was situated at the farthest point possible from the front door. What's the big deal? Kids being kids, I was punched, kicked, and called a retard or worse every time I walked up and down that hallway, and I was required to walk that hallway several times a day "running the gauntlet"[7]

The punishment that my classmates and I received daily at the hands of the other students in that school was relentless, inescapable, and seldom hindered by the faculty. One of my classmates, who I will call Bob, was a few years older than me. He came to school one day drunk and waving a handgun around when he got off the bus. Needless to say, his behavior earned him faculty intervention very quickly. He was taken to the office. As I think back on the situation, it is almost incomprehensible that adults would allow what happened next to occur, never mind those who are trained educators.

While they were holding Bob and waiting for the police to arrive, they kept him in the front area of the office, which was separated from the main entrance hall and cafeteria by huge glass windows. Bob was dancing around the office and making obscene gestures and screaming at the horde of students that had assembled on the other side of the glass. I will never forget the expression on his

---

[7] Running the gauntlet—a medieval practice of making a person found guilty of a crime or infraction run between rows of people who mercilessly strike and attack.

face. This is the type of situation that is not soon forgotten, even considering my lack of recall during most of my childhood. Many of the little video clips bouncing around in my head are from disturbing events. His expression was of joy. He was smiling and laughing like he thoroughly enjoyed the attention.

Soon the kids in the hallway were worked up into a frenzy; beating on the windows, and screaming obscenities. It's amazing the glass didn't break. They were like a pack of wild animals. A few in the crowd noticed a friend and me standing a little way down the hallway. Within moments they were screaming at us, "There are some of the retards!" Before we had a chance escape, we were surrounded. All we could do was curl up in the fetal position and wait for the beating to end.

That was the last time any of us saw Bob, but it wasn't the first or the last time we were beaten in such a manner. It was a regular occurrence. The boys' locker room was a real treat before and after gym class. Yes, for some reason, someone decided it would be a good idea that we attend gym class along with the rest of the students. We ate lunch, went to recess, and rode the bus to and from school with the other kids as well. Most of us would have done anything to fit in and be considered cool.

None of us considered learning as having anything to do with our "sentence" at East Hampton Junior High. We were there for survival training, which was more like incarceration than education. Sometimes we were invited to participate in activities by the other kids as a way of showing we were cool. It often involved smoking pot or cigarettes or some type of sexually perverse activity. Most of the time, these invitations were nothing more than set-ups for more humiliation.

One of my friends had a paper route. I would often walk along with him as he delivered the newspapers. One day we were walking through the graveyard that ran adjacent to our neighborhood when we stopped to smoke a cigarette. The cemetery was a common shortcut and a place we often hung out to do the things that we shouldn't have been doing. As we were standing there, a group of older boys came along and started talking to us. They must have noticed we were just puffing on the cigarettes and not inhaling.

Being only nine or ten years old, we had no idea what we were doing. The only thing we knew was that it was cool to smoke. They asked if we knew how to inhale, and, of course, we said we did. They knew we were full of crap and told us to take a big puff from our cigarettes, so we did, and then they said that wasn't enough and to puff more, so we did it again. Then they told us to breathe in as hard as we could. Holy shit, it felt like a knife ripping through my chest. We both got dizzy and couldn't stand. The older kids thought this was hysterical. They laughed, repeatedly kicking us, landing several blows to our faces and heads until we were bloody.

When I was twelve years old, my family moved to the town of Westbrook, Connecticut. I saw this as my big chance for a new start, and I came out of the chute like a bucking bronco. As the kids would say today, I wasn't going to let anyone "disrespect me" for any reason. If someone said something to me that I thought was belittling, I was ready to fight. This didn't turn out to be a very good plan. I was angry and had a chip on my shoulder, but I was a bit of a geek. I was tall and thin. I don't think I could have done a single pushup at the time. I use the term "geek" lovingly. I'm still a bit of a geek, and if you don't believe me, ask my children. Although I'm a little stronger than I was in those days, I love my electronic gadgets and am a bit of a bookworm.

As it turns out, when you end up getting the crap

kicked out of you by most of the kids who you challenge, it does little to solidify your reputation as one of the cool kids in town. I was immediately placed in special education classes upon arriving at my new school. The hope I had for a new beginning was not realized. Nothing changed, and I was still considered, as I was reminded almost daily by most of the other children, one of the "retards."

I was terribly unhappy and lived in such a constant state of fear that I developed ticks. I twitched constantly, either blinking my eyes excessively, jerking my head back and forth, or making grunting noises, all of which are behaviors associated with Tourette's syndrome, which gave the kids at school, even more ammunition to humiliate me on a daily basis.

An older boy who I knew in town started hanging around with me and eventually talked me into performing oral sex on him. As I have mentioned, I would have done anything to receive someone's approval. For years I never realized that what this boy did to me could be considered sexual abuse because he compelled me to go along with his desires. He asked me regularly if I could ejaculate. I had not gone through puberty, so the answer was always no.

I thought there was something wrong with me. I spent hours masturbating, convinced that if I could just ejaculate, this boy would think I was cool. Talk about the epitome of codependent behavior. This boy was sexually abusing me, and I was damn near wearing the skin off my penis because I was ashamed that I couldn't ejaculate. I masturbated so much that my penis bled on several occasions. Codependency is an issue that I address in detail in chapter six.

This went on for over a year. The last few times it happened, the boy became rough with me. The last time it happened was at my house. I was home alone, and he came over. We began doing what we had done so many times before, and he started hurting me. I was scared and tried pulling away. The more I pulled away, the more he forced me. I finally broke away from him and ran down the stairs. He was right on my heels. I ran out our back door, and as I did, he slammed the door on my leg. I screamed in pain and fell out onto the back porch. As I lay there crying, he stepped over me and walked out.

That was the last time he molested me, but it was not my last shameful interaction with him.

Before I continue my story, I want to spend the next four chapters going over some of the nuts and bolts of PTSD, covering the topics of dissociation, physical changes to the minds of sexual abuse victims, hypervigilance, and codependency.

Chapter 3

Dissociation

> Without realizing it, I fought to keep my two worlds separated. Without ever knowing why, I made sure, whenever possible that nothing passed between the compartmentalization I had created between the day child and the night child."
>
> —Marilyn Van Derbur,
> *Miss America by Day*

> The conflict between the will to deny horrible events and the will to proclaim them aloud is the central dialectic of psychological trauma.
>
> —Judith Lewis Herman,
> *Trauma and Recovery: The Aftermath of Violence— From Domestic Abuse to Political Terror*

As I touched on, in the last chapter, throughout this book I will discuss terms such as post-traumatic stress disorder (PTSD), hypervigilance, disassociation, adverse childhood experiences (ACE), and codependency. As we delve into the science of mental health and particularly the issue of PTSD, it becomes clear that there are many gray areas. These terms are not absolutes. They are simply words used to identify unhealthy cognitive, emotional, and behavioral patterns often associated with traumatic stress or other adverse circumstances in a person's life or development. If we were to look at these terms in the form of a stained-glass window, the different sections would not be separated by nice neat lead partitions (camework). The edges of each section would be infused and blended and quite often not just at the edges but also deep within the sections.

As we delve into this issue, I feel it necessary to begin by pointing out that dissociation is often misunderstood. Many who hear the word automatically think of split personality disorder, or as it is called today, dissociative identity disorder (DID). Unfortunately, this disorder has been sensationalized by the media and in fiction. Few hear the name "Sybil" and don't think of the 1973 book of the same name written by Flora Rheta Schreiber, which quickly climbed the bestseller list and was eventually made into two television movies. The book was supposedly written about a psychiatric patient named Shirley Mason who suffered from "multiple personality disorder." Shirley Mason later admitted that she faked her disorder.[1]

The public has become fascinated with dissociation, and that interest has provided tremendous fodder for the entertainment industry. There is no shortage of horror films and thrillers whose main protagonists exhibit DID in an extreme and unrealistic manner. Hollywood has lined its pockets due to the public's appetite for the misunderstood, gory, and extraordinary. Unfortunately, many in the mental health community have grabbed hold of this disorder for the same reasons. The reality is that most mental health professionals go through their entire careers seeing few, if any, actual cases of DID. The unfortunate result of the attention that dissociation has received is that it all too often comes packed with a negative stig-

---

[1] Lynn Neary, "Real 'Sybil' Admits Multiple Personalities Were Fake," *National Public Radio,* October 20, 2011, https://www.npr.org/2011/10/20/141514464/real-sybil-admits-multiple-personalities-were-fake.

ma.

Although dissociation can be an issue for concern, it is more common than people realize. Most people experience dissociative symptoms from time to time. Some of the more common symptoms are déjà vu,[2] small memory glitches, or a feeling that a situation is surreal or out of context.[3] Dissociation manifests itself in countless ways both acutely and chronically. As the mental health community learns more about this disorder, more and more practitioners are realizing it's quite common.

Let's take a look at what Dr. Bessel van der Kolk says about the reason for dissociation.

> Dissociation is the essence of trauma. The overwhelming experience is split off and fragmented, so that the emotions, sounds, images, thoughts, and physical sensations related to the trauma take on a life of their own. The sensory fragments of memory intrude into the present, where they are literally relived. As long as the trauma is not resolved, the stress hormones that the body secretes to protect itself keep circulating, and the defensive movements and emotional responses keep getting replayed.[4]

The faces, feelings, and attitudes of dissociation are many. Sufferers often appear subdued, melancholy, zoned out with the thousand-yard stare, or depressed. At other times it may manifest as a misunderstood expression, agitation, sleep-deprivation, or the feeling of being uncomfortable in one's own skin. These fragmented emotions and thoughts may also surface as unexplained and often misunderstood emotional outbursts of anger, resentment,

---

[2] Fredrick Neuman, "A theory of Deja Vu and Jamais Vu," *Psychology Today*, January 1, 2013, https://www.psychologytoday.com/us/blog/fighting-fear/201301/theory-deja-vu-and-jamais-vu.
[3] Bessel van der Kolk, *The Body Keeps the Score: Brain, Mind, and Body in the Healing of Trauma* (New Your, NY: Penguin, 2015), 123.
[4] Ibid., 66.

or fear—the often misunderstood, disturbing, and at times downright confrontational and seemingly unmanageable faces of dissociation.[5]

Many in the mental health community teach that our minds use three main avenues to deal with trauma through our autonomic nervous system: fight, flight, or freeze. Fight and flight are commonly understood as our natural inclination to either stand and fight or run away when we're afraid or facing a traumatic event.[6] Maybe not so commonly understood is the freeze response, which is often theorized as being a primal defense, somehow developed through the evolutionary process. This response is often equated with reptiles or other animals that have learned to "play dead" as a response to being attacked or threatened by a predator. Another way that this is displayed in the animal kingdom, as well as in humans, is the inclination to stand still or freeze with the hope of not being confronted or noticed.[7]

Some associate "checking out" or freezing with our mind's natural ability to deal with trauma or stress. I'm not sure I agree. I don't believe that physically or mentally, checking out is natural in any way. When faced with an inability to exercise the desired and natural inclination (i.e., need) to fight or run, the mind shuts down—much like a computer freezing when its processing capacity is overloaded. This is not a natural adaptation; it is maladaptive.

A child being restrained during abuse will shut down and withdraw, his or her mind taking the child someplace else—anyplace other than in the present moment. Being involved in an auto accident or the horrors of war are other examples of situations in which people can become

---

[5] Ibid., 66–68.
[6] Ibid., 82.
[7] Peter Levine, *Walking The Tiger: Healing Trauma* (Berkley, California: North Atlantic Books, 1997), 18-20.

overwhelmed. Most can relate to the phrase "scared stupid" or "scared senseless." This numbing or checking out can also develop as the result of long-term abuse.

For many of us, when our minds first learn to check out or go numb is when dissociation is born. This is when the "fragments of memory" described by Dr. van der Kolk in the quote above break free. These fragments become the floating debris that lies just beneath the surface of our consciousness, waiting to be rediscovered so they can pull us back to a place we have so desperately tried to forget. When we begin to feel this pull, our minds once again take us anyplace but to what we have learned to forget—we dissociate. Dissociation comes in many forms, as I will discuss as we move along.

These fragments of memory are often referred to as triggers: certain smells, something someone says or does, a news article, and so on. Sometimes nothing more than another person's attitude or posture can send us into a tailspin.[8]

An important key to recovery is becoming aware of our emotions. One of the biggest stumbling blocks toward healing from dissociation is disassociation from ourselves. It is next to impossible to understand what we feel unless we are aware of our emotions. This may sound like double talk, but it is true. I spent years not just avoiding my emotions but running as hard as I could from them. Once we stop running, it can become overwhelming, whether we stop by choice or because we have run out of steam, and our past overtakes us with a vengeance. Whichever way, we need help, and the road to recovery can be long and confusing at times but worth the effort.

It may not always be the case, but I believe that most people are fully aware of what is happening during dissociative episodes, even if they have no idea why it's hap-

---

[8] van der Kolk, *The Body Keeps Score,* 110.

pening. This is true for subtle instances, such as memory glitches and the feeling that something is surreal, as well as for outbursts of anger and unexplained fits of crying. Most can relate to comments like "I don't know what comes over me; I just get so angry sometimes" or "What's wrong with me? I start crying over the littlest things." Sometimes we get so overwhelmed that we decide to "just go with it." There are times when our lives become so unmanageable that we just snap. That's what happened to me when I was standing in the middle of the road, drunk out of my mind, completely naked, and screaming into the night like a lunatic.

Never once during those episodes did I lose consciousness of who I was or what I was doing. What I have come close to losing during those times, however, is hope. Keep in mind that as long as we have enough fight left in us that we are screaming into the night, we are still clinging to hope. It's when we stop fighting that we should be concerned.

It is never good when we become so undone that unrestrained emotions pour forth in torrents of anguish or anger, but it happens. We can become overwhelmed or just plain sick of feeling depressed, misunderstood, or angry because our lives have been hijacked by something from our past that was altogether beyond our control. Sometimes the feeling of melancholy, frustration, the pain of the past, the despair of the future, and the feeling of being completely and utterly unattached becomes unacceptable for even one more moment.

At such times many of us can relate to watching, the "other us" spring onto the scene like a long-awaited hero or villain. This is the part of ourselves that should have come to our rescue but remained fettered with misplaced apprehension. I say "hero" or "villain" because we are not sure if this "other us" will bring liberty or destruction, but as we sit by watching the scene unfold, many of us can relate to the feeling that either is welcome.

I have heard such displays of unrestrained emotion described as, or blamed on, a dissociative break—an episode when we become completely unaware of our behavior. Such outbreaks are so disturbing because most of us are aware of what is happening. It is not only our behavior that seems utterly surreal and unrelatable but also our emotions. I look at these moments as a culmination of reality and emotions that should have been expressed over a lifetime but instead have been bottled up in a dark corner of our hearts. When they finally come forth, it is neither pretty nor clean.

It is much easier to deny any knowledge of the existence of our "other self" than acknowledge our feelings and behavior. This dilemma, inability, or refusal to be honest with ourselves and the world around us is the essence of dissociation. The problem with acknowledging our other self is that many of us have spent the better part of a lifetime trying to ignore its existence.

This other self is the part of us that has been banished to the dark recesses of our heart along with all of the fragmented traumatic memories and emotions of our past. When this other self cries out, we comprehend every sob and share in its languished breath, though many people feign ignorance. What we find most disturbing is that we understand all too well that we are just as much this other self as we are the "self" we chose to share with "polite society."

Although this other self is safely locked away, we hear its mournful cries in the quiet of the night. At first we learn to squelch these cries with the noise of the world and the chaos of life. As time slips by, these lonely, shameful cries continue to drift into the chambers of our hearts. Instead of becoming subdued, they become more pervasive. The other self that we have tried desperately to keep hidden away somehow gains liberty as its yearning entangles itself with the very fabric of our lives. Though the lock remains secure, it has somehow learned to inhabit our subconscious mind through the look of a stranger, the attitude of a parent or colleague, or the words of a friend. This other self has learned to invade our senses through everyday events and inhabits our dreams.

Before long we learn to numb our senses in an effort to quiet the cries by drinking alcohol, taking drugs, becoming addicted to sex or pornography, overeating, and so on. At first we are comforted by these diversions, feeling they are exactly what we need to relieve the pain and quiet the noise in our heads.

What we do not anticipate, however, is that during our anesthetized state, we become helpless against the beckoning sobs of this banished other self. In time we find ourselves standing at the door of the chamber in which we locked away this poor, wretched, helpless half-soul so long ago. As the numbing effects of our addiction begin to fade, we run from this door, vowing never to return. The shame, pain, and helplessness are more than we can bear.

But we do return, time and again—standing, waiting, listening. Soon we find ourselves touching the door as we lean against the chill of the slab, longing for the slightest whisper. That which we fear the most becomes inescapable. One day we find ourselves standing at the door holding the key.

This story plays out every day in the lives of many of us who have been traumatized. Several endings can be written to this story. The first, most grievous, and all too common is that we die as the result of our addiction, never having the opportunity to turn the key in the lock. How many die every day of a drug overdose, cirrhosis of the liver, cancer, AIDS, obesity, a tragic accident, or suicide?

Whether people take their own lives, suffer the ravages alcoholism or drug addiction, or die in some type of accident, they all die from the same cause. The face looking back in the mirror is the same. Our stories may differ, but we all fight the same inner demons.

All too often we decide to face our other self in the heat of our addiction. This is a path that I walked for way too long. When I turned the key in the lock, the bolt clanked free, and the door swung open, I was overcome with a torrent of emotion for which I was utterly unprepared. I dove headlong into my addiction, trying to kill the pain, and when I surfaced from time to time in sobriety, I was overcome with shame.

I had no idea what I was feeling or how to stop the pain. I was a drowning man. I was tormenting myself, but what is worse, I was tormenting everyone around me. I destroyed relationships with my unpredictable, unreasonable, and turbulent behavior. Life became a cycle of intoxication and seemingly never-ending confrontations and arguments. How can we begin to heal when we refuse to acknowledge or articulate what we are fighting?

The best way for this story to end is by going to the door in sobriety, armed with the truth, and if at all possible with a friend (a counselor) who can help us get back on our feet when we become overcome with shame and anger. This way when we turn the key, the door opens, and we are faced with our "other self," we will have a chance of responding and being received in love (compassion). We will still undoubtedly be overwhelmed at times with unexpected and misunderstood emotion, but the truth will set us free. We may stumble from time to time, but we need to have the presence of mind in sobriety to get back up and face what we don't understand. No longer drowning in raw turbulent, and misunderstood emotion, but learning to feel, become aware of, and gain an understanding of the subtle undercurrents. When we learn to feel in truth, we become fully alive.

The healing process can be life-changing. In many regards I have found it to be fulfilling and even enjoyable. When we learn to embrace our past and stand armed with the truth, we are free to crack open the door to life and all its fullness (John 10:10). I realize you may not feel ready to face your past, never mind embrace it, but hang on. Just the fact that you are reading this book is evidence that you are headed in the right direction. The road to healing is not straight. It has its ups and downs, rough patches, and straightaways. You will stumble and even fall at times. But stumbling toward the light is better than sliding numbly into darkness. I will discuss healing in much greater detail as we move along.

Depersonalization and derealization are subheadings or subcategories of dissociation. The mental health community developed these terms to help us get a better understanding of the symptoms. They have also helped deflect some of the negative stigma associated with dissociation.

Depersonalization and derealization can also be referred to as depersonalization-derealization disorder. As time goes by, other subgroups or headings may be established. Our understanding of dissociation is in its infancy, as with much of our knowledge of the mind.

The following can be found on the Mayo Clinic website:[9]

Symptoms of depersonalization include:

---

[9] "Depersonalization-derealization disorder" Mayo Clinic, https://www.mayoclinic.org/diseases-conditions/depersonalization-derealization-disorder/symptoms-causes/syc-20352911.

- Feelings that you're an outside observer of your thoughts, feelings, your body or parts of your body — for example, as if you were floating in air above yourself

- Feeling like a robot or that you're not in control of your speech or movements

- The sense that your body, legs or arms appear distorted, enlarged or shrunken, or that your head is wrapped in cotton

- Emotional or physical numbness of your senses or responses to the world around you

- A sense that your memories lack emotion, and that they may or may not be your own memories

Symptoms of derealization include:

- Feelings of being alienated from or unfamiliar with your surroundings — for example, like you're living in a movie or a dream

- Feeling emotionally disconnected from people you care about, as if you were separated by a glass wall

- Surroundings that appear distorted, blurry, colorless, two-dimensional or artificial, or a heightened awareness and clarity of your surroundings

- Distortions in perception of time, such as recent events feeling like distant past

- Distortions of distance and the size and shape of objects

As discussed above in the stained-glass window analogy, the terminology, symptoms, and issues concerned are not clear-cut and often overlap, blend, and intertwine. I found that it was helpful when trying to get my head wrapped around this issue not to get caught up in trying to identify my symptoms or manifestations within different categories or looking for a definitive diagnosis.

Most important to healing is not to let yourself get upset or stressed out when symptoms occur. Think of the manifestations or symptoms as your mind's way of letting you know that it needs relief. Many of these symptoms can be short episodes while others can last for long periods of time—hours, weeks, months—or in some cases become a way of life.

Getting stressed out when we experience symptoms will most likely do nothing more than exacerbate the situation and can often lead to physical complications such as panic or anxiety attacks, of which I am no stranger. Once we begin to understand what is happening, the important part is to acknowledge the issue without shame or fear and begin the steps toward healing.

Some of the symptoms of dissociation that I have experienced are listed below. Your symptoms may be similar, which is why I'm sharing this list. This is a large part of why I have written this book. Some of my most significant strides toward healing have happened when relating another person's testimony and what they have experienced on their path toward recovery. There is great comfort in understanding that we are not alone. I spent many years isolating myself because I thought I was fatally flawed when the truth is that I am just one of the countless thousands making the same journey.

- Zoning out or checking out: When this occurs, I go into a state of unawareness. I'm not sure where my mind goes, and I often have no perception of how long it occurs. As I described in the last chapter, it often requires some type of physical stimulation to break me out of this state: a loud noise, a tap on the shoulder, and so forth. Typically when I break out of this state, I have no idea where I am or what I'm doing and often no awareness of self. The breaking-out period only lasts for five to ten seconds at most, and I am back to myself.
- Feeling as though my arms are not my own. I watch my arms, and I feel as though they are doing their own thing.
- Feeling like I am living in a dream. It typically only lasts for seconds or minutes. It is tangible, like walking through a door, and everything changes. Then, just as suddenly, the feeling subsides.
- Difficulty perceiving or having a feeling of the future.
- I have had several recurring dreams for as long as I can remember. The first is being naked and facing the fact that I need to go out in public. I don't usually get to the point where I go into public in the dream, but it does happen. The dream seems to be more about the dilemma. The second dream is about feeling as though I need to run, but I can't

move my legs fast enough or at all. It's almost like they are made of lead or that they won't respond no matter what I do. It's a terrifying and helpless feeling. The third is snakes. The odd thing about this dream is that I have little fear of snakes while I'm awake. In my dreams what's so frightening is the quantity—the snakes are coming at me in overwhelming numbers. The idea that dreams are associated with dissociation is gaining ground in the mental health community.[10]

- Becoming angry, upset, or overwhelmed with a situation or person for no apparent reason. I have never had the desire to hurt anyone. My typical response is to withdraw, shut down, and at times become sad to the point of tears.
- Weeping for no apparent reason.
- Becoming incensed at the drop of a hat if I feel backed into a corner, shamed, or belittled. I have never lashed out at anyone physically, but I feel the need to stand my ground at times and have startled people with a harsh verbal response. It can be forceful, immediate, and all too often regrettable.
- Unable to recall everyday things—names, places, and events, typically, when I perceive that I am being hurried for the answer. These are often things that I should be able to remember as well as my own name.
- Being unable to remember parts of my childhood.
- Déjà vu, which is a sense that something has already happened or a feeling of familiarity with a place or a situation that we are experiencing for

---

[10] Petr Bob and Olga Louchakova, "Dissociative states in dreams and brain chaos: implications for creative awareness," *Perspective*, September 7, 2015, https://www.frontiersin.org/articles/10.3389/fpsyg.2015.01353/full.

the first time.

As I began to explain above, when trying to understand this issue it's helpful not to get caught up in trying to identify individual symptoms or manifestations within a specific category (depersonalization or derealization) or to look for a definitive diagnosis. We are not trying to heal particular symptoms but focusing on healing the underlying reasons for the condition. Once we learn to understand what we feel, and how to take back our lives from the memories of our past and anxiety concerning the future, the symptoms of dissociation will begin to subside.

One of the fears/questions that I dealt with concerning dissociation was, "What if I start remembering, and what if those memories are things that I would prefer not to deal with?" This concern is valid. If dissociation involves displaced and fragmented memories and emotions, then it stands to reason that as we begin to resolve our issues, some of our memories and emotions will fall back into place. At times this can happen, but it is not always the case. This is one of reason why I encourage anyone working through issues of dissociation to do so with the help of a trained and licensed counselor.

Some of us may recall memories or feelings associated with our childhood. Typically, these memories do not return as a fully developed narrative of past events. Quite often they return as fragmented scenes or bodily sensations. Many are more like feelings—something tugging on the periphery of your consciousness.

This is how it has happened for me and is still happening. I have brief memories that are more like single framed glimpses that pass through my consciousness. They are more emotional than visual. To be frank, they are uncomfortable and perplexing at times. Some are nothing more than bodily sensations brought on by certain situations or physical positions.

I understand that my descriptions may be a little vague. I am attempting to describe something that is almost abstract. You will most likely understand if this is something that you have gone through or experienced. Many of these memories or sensations may be valid, but it's possible they are nothing more than our misunderstanding of past events. Avoid drawing conclusions until these memories develop into full narratives that fit into your past.

The problem with fragmented memories is that they can become altered and unreliable. Many of us have memories of abuse that we have never forgotten—memories that are indelibly imprinted in our minds. These are not the memories to which I am referring. Be careful of anyone trying to convince that those memories are unreliable. I am talking about the memories that have been long forgotten but one day begin to surface unannounced. These memories can be valid, but not always, especially if your past involves pornography or inappropriate sexual behavior. Those who have such a history have countless fragmented and inappropriate images bouncing around in their heads that are subject to resurface at any time. Some theorize that our minds store every memory, dream, and bodily sensation that we have ever experienced.

Donna Jackson Nakazawa, in her book, *Child Disrupted: How Your Biography Becomes Your Biology, and How You Can Heal*, writes:

> Most people consider powerful memories to be like snapshots or video clips that we can review and replay, and assume our memories are a true rendition of the past.
>
> But those captured memories actually get re-

vised all our lives. Even after a memory has been consolidated—encoded and stored in our amygdala and hippocampus—it doesn't stay consolidated. Our brain rewrites those memories over time, based on new information and experiences. Each time we remember an incident of childhood adversity, that particular memory becomes labile, or susceptible to changes in how and what we remember about what happened.[11]

At one time, I had a particular image coming into my memory. I had no idea where it came from—it was nothing more than a glimpse. I spent months worrying about if it was associated with past abuse. One day I was looking through an old family photo album and came across a picture of that image. My concerns and worry immediately evaporated. It was merely an image that I had seen long ago but had forgotten. We need to be careful to treat such images or feelings with a degree of skepticism. I am not saying our first impulse should be to deny our past or distrust our memories, but we should wade into such issues with caution.

Another fear that I had concerning recalling forgotten memories is what to do with them. I guess I had some preconceived notion of child abuse victims confronting their abusers in some type of dramatic grandstand even in the name of correcting the wrong. Let me dismiss that fear right now. I have never confronted any of my abusers. We are not on a crusade or a witch hunt. Recovery is not about confronting your past; it is about dealing with your past. There is a vast difference. Recovery is about finally learning to leave your past where it belongs—in the past and becoming fully alive to the peasant.

---

[11] Donna Jackson Nakazawa, *Childhood Disrupted: How Your Biography Becomes Your Biology, and How You Can Heal* (New York, NY: Atria, 2015), 84.

There is a time for us to share your past and all of your memories, but it should not be with our abusers. I will get into how to share your past in a healthy and healing way in the pages ahead, but for now just understand that your recovery is your recovery. It is about you and no one else, and that's OK. There is nothing wrong with having a little "me time."

Some of us may feel the impulse or desire to confront our abusers, especially if they are a close family member, such as a parent or sibling. You may be ready to do that one day, but there is a time when you need to focus on yourself. If you decide to confront such a person, you want to do it in the right spirit and on your terms. There is no legitimate reason why you should feel compelled to discuss your abuse with your abuser other than out of a desire to continue in relationship with that person. I say this with some trepidation. Such relationships should only be pursued once we are strong enough to maintain healthy boundaries, preferably with the assistance of a trusted counselor.

Many feel the need to confront an abuser out of an assortment of feelings, such as misplaced guilt, fear, anger, vengeance, sympathy, or a desire to set the record straight. All of these are the wrong reasons and are instead evidence that we need time to heal. By urging you not to confront your abuser, I am not telling you to run or hide from your past. Instead, it is a way of taking control of your life.

When you feel compelled to confront your abuser in such a way, you are fostering confusion and giving power to the enemy. You need to understand that your abuser is not the enemy! Once you learn to stop viewing your abuser as the enemy, you remove that person's power over you. Your true struggle is with the stronghold that that was created in your mind by trauma. By focusing on your abuser, you are taking your eyes off of the real problem. If you are currently in an abusive situation, it needs to stop immediately. Once you are free and in a safe place physically, it is time to take control of your life and learn to dwell in a safe place emotionally.

I understand that many people are not in a place where they feel that they will ever be free of their abusive past. Many people feel this way because they are focusing on the end goal and not the journey—they are looking up at a mountain that seems insurmountable. I find it helpful to simply focus on the next step. The next step may be your first. Here is how the first step goes—take a deep breath and exhale, and slowly and say to yourself, "Everything may not be okay today, but one day it will."

An essential aspect of recovery is self-reliance. Self-reliance is a common thread that you will find running throughout this book and in most credible discussions concerning the healing of trauma. Another common thread that you will encounter throughout my writing is reliance on God. These two concepts may seem contradictory. Throughout biblical history, seldom did God ever fight someone's battles. God does help us fight our battles, but He most often does not do the fighting while we cower on the sidelines (see Joshua 1:19, Isaiah 41:10, Deuteronomy 31:6, Zephaniah, 3:17, Psalm 23, Matthew 28:20, and Hebrews 13:5). Here is the thing about taking God by the hand—He will most assuredly walk you through the fire (Daniel 3) and through the valley of the shadow of death (Psalm 23:4).

God's Word makes it clear that God is not interested in coddling His children. It has been my experience that His interests lie in helping His children develop character, which can only be achieved by walking through the hard places in life. The Bible does not direct readers toward a walk down Easy Street. Instead, it is a book full of stories of God walking with his children through situations that seem insurmountable.

God doesn't ever promise to do the work for us, but He does promise to be with us and love us without limits. Let me caution you: if you take God by the hand, you are taking hold of the hand of a person who loves you enough that He will never let you sit on the sidelines and give up. He will lead you back out into the battle every time. It is His Spirit that keeps us from flailing in the dark by illuminating our path and allowing us to see our true adversary. He knows that we need to have a firm grip on the hilt of the blade that vanquishes the enemy. To the victor go the spoils!

Chapter 4

The Change

> [to her baby] Did you have a nightmare? I have nightmares too. Someday I'll explain it to you. Why they came. Why they won't ever go away. But I'll tell you how I survive it. I make a list in my head. Of all the good things I've seen someone do. Every little thing I could remember. It's like a game. I do it over and over. Gets a little tedious after all these years, but . . . There are much worse games to play.
>
> —Katniss Everdeen, *The Hunger Games*

Many of us who are dealing with the emotional issues associated with traumatic stress have heard someone say to us at one time or another "You need to learn to get past this" or "You need to forgive, forget, and move on." I heard these sentiments long before I ever considered that I was suffering from PTSD. I wish it were that easy. I have heard them from pastors at church and mental health counselors. Why couldn't I just simply "get past" the guilt, pain, shame, and my endless propensity to allow myself to be hurt by others? Why couldn't I just get past being offended by what might seem to others to be the stupidest things?

Let me help you. There is no way to just "get past" PTSD. It is a disorder like few others. We could approach this disorder with the fatalistic approach that we are irreversibly broken—a sentiment spoken and written by many addressing this issue. I prefer to think of us as changed. As you will learn, we have been irrefutably and irreversibly changed by trauma. However, this change does not need to be our end or our undoing. On the contrary, if we will allow it, this change can help us live a life bolstered by our better qualities. This may be difficult to understand at this point in your journey—I hope it becomes a little clearer as we move along.

When I began dealing with the issue of PTSD, life became an exploration of my emotions. Several years into my recovery, I began to understand that what I was dealing with was not merely emotional. I wish I had understood the physical aspects of traumatic stress from the beginning. What I did not understand is that the "disorder" aspect of PTSD is neurological as well as emotional. Without the neurological aspect, it is not a disorder. It is as cut and as dried as that. This is what many people, including many mental health clinicians, fail to understand. It is not an emotional state that one can simply "move past." As Donna Jackson Nakazawa explains in her book, *Childhood Disrupted: How Your Biography becomes Your Biology, and How You Can Heal,*

> New findings in neuroscience, psychology, and medicine have recently unveiled the exact ways in which childhood adversity biologically alters us for life. This groundbreaking research tells us that the emotional trauma we face when we are young has farther-reaching consequences than we might have imagined. Adverse Childhood Experiences change the architecture of our brains and the health of our immune systems, they trigger and sustain inflammation in both body and brain, and they influence our overall physical health and longevity long into

adulthood.[1]

Let me explain further. Our bodies are controlled and regulated by our nervous system. Our nervous system is complex and in many ways still being explored. In the past ten to twenty years there has been a renaissance of sorts in the field of neurology. Just in the four years since I wrote the first draft of this chapter, it seems that almost daily, new information has been made available. We are learning that the inner workings of our nervous system are more complex and awe inspiring than we ever realized—how this amazing system affects our health, and how our health affects our nervous system.

Think of our nervous system as two different systems, the somatic and autonomic. In some ways these two systems work independent of each other, and in other ways they work together. We can think of the somatic nervous[2] system as being responsible for voluntary movements of the body. For example, if I would like a sip of coffee, I must tell my arm and hand to reach over, grab the cup, and bring it to my mouth. Then I need to tell my mouth to take a sip.

The second system is the autonomic nervous system (ANS). This is the system that I will be focusing on during the remainder of this chapter. The autonomic system is responsible for the regulation and control of all of our involuntary needs.

The ANS is further broken down into two systems working in concert to regulate the needs of the body, the SNS (sympathetic nervous system) and the PSNS (parasympathetic nervous system). One of the responsibilities of the SNS that I did not include in my list above is that it

---

[1] Donna Jackson Nakazawa, *Childhood Disrupted: How Your Biography Becomes Your Biology, and How You Can Heal* (New York: Atria, 2015), 9–10.
[2] Micky A. Akinrodoye and Forshing Lue, "Neuroanatomy, Somatic Nervous System," *StatePearls*, April 2, 2020, https://www.ncbi.nlm.nih.gov/books/NBK556027/.

orchestrates our fight-or-flight response. This is the mechanism that releases that extra burst of adrenaline when it is needed. It gives our bodies the desire and the energy required during times of stress—when it is time to get up and go or stay and fight.

The SNS regulates muscle tension as related to blood flow and likewise affects blood pressure and regulates other bodily functions, such as pupil dilation, perspiration, heart rate, respiration, and the release of sexual hormones. The SNS system can be somewhat influenced by a conscious choice. We can stimulate the SNS by going for a run or participating in other physical exercise to increase the release of adrenalin.

The PSNS is a little more difficult to manage with behavior. The PSNS dials things back down after adrenaline has amped up our system. It also controls our involuntary process, such as circulation, kidney function, and digestion. We can think of it as the system that keeps us balanced.

When your heart rate increases due to a release of adrenalin (a stress hormone), it is your PSNS that slows your heart back down once the need for increased performance has passed. One of the only bodily functions that we can consciously control that helps in regaining synchronicity of the ANS is breathing. No conscious choice is required to breathe, which is a good thing. Otherwise, when we go to sleep, we would stop breathing. However, we can choose at any time to suspend breathing or to take a few deep breaths. This ability, in turn, gives us one of the few ways that we can help regain balance between the SNS and PSNS. When we inhale, the heart is controlled by the SNS, which increases our heart rate. When we exhale, the PNS takes over, decreasing our heart rate. This is why it is so helpful to take a few deep, heavy breaths before beginning strenuous exercise. It increases oxygen levels and our heart rate and gives us a shot of adrenaline.

Likewise, we can engage the PSNS by taking a few deep breaths while focusing on a lengthened outbreath. When we take in a short, deep breath and then release it with a long, slow exhale, it stimulates the PSNS, relaxing the body. This is a technique that we can use to help in healing the ANS or simply to calm down after a stressful situation.[3]

Many of the functions of our PSNS are controlled by the brain through the vagus nerve, which is the tenth cranial nerve. There are also other parasympathetic nerves, such as the third cranial or oculomotor nerve (eye function) and the sacral nerves (pelvic nerves).[4] The vagus nerve is the largest and carries information to and from the brain, running from the cranium to the abdomen with branches that extend to the organs of the body.

Inflammation affecting the vagus nerve is one of the primary causes of the disruption of the ANS. I have combed through countless publications and read phrases like "we now understand" or "we are beginning to understand." In other words, we are learning new things about the ANS every day.

The vagus nerve can affect and be affected by our health for many reasons. For example, the digestive system can become inflamed or disrupted because of damage to the vagus nerve.[5] The vagus nerve runs right along the esophagus and is attached to the stomach. Acid reflux or a hiatal hernia can greatly affect or even damage the

---

[3] Bessel van der Kolk, *The Body Keeps the Score: Brain, Mind, and Body in the Healing of Trauma* (New Your, NY: Penguin, 2015), 79.
[4] Timothy C Hain, "Dysautonomia," Dizzyness-and-balance.com, April 7, 2019, https://dizziness-and-balance.com/disorders/medical/dysautonomia.html.
[5] "Gastroparesis," *Mayo Clinic*, https://www.mayoclinic.org/diseases-conditions/gastroparesis/symptoms-causes/syc-20355787.

vagus nerve.[6]

For those who suffer from PTSD, the vagus nerve can be affected by years of being marinated in stress hormones. This inflammation can and will affect the body's organs. It is common for someone who has PTSD to report, for example, heart issues, gastrointestinal discomfort, or irritable bowel syndrome, never to receive a proper diagnosis.[7]

Four years ago when I began this book, I thought I felt pretty good. Mentally, I had put my past behind me and was moving on with my life. As I explained in the introduction, I received several comments from readers after reading *Purgatory: Heaven's Healing Waters,* that they felt there was another book to be written about my past and my path to recovery. I was not sure I was ready, but it felt like the right time. Like so many things, we need to listen to when God says to move and let Him worry about the details. I had no idea this work would be just as much about my healing as it is about sharing my story in a book.

Soon after I started, I began having bouts of anxiety and a laundry list of other physical issues. I had no idea what was happening. I didn't feel too terribly upset about what I was writing, but evidently, my mind was having a hard time understanding that I was OK. The anxiety started out mild and mounted. Within a month or so, it was so severe that it was keeping me up at night. I would be awakened in the middle of the night by the sound of my pulse pounding in my ears, more often than not accompanied by palpitations that felt like my heart was doing somersaults in my chest. I would jump up out of bed,

---

[6] Steve Rochlitz, "A missing link to chronic illness, allergies and longevity? Vagus Nerve Imbalance/Hiatal Hernia Syndrome," *The Townsend Letter Group*, August–September 2003,
https://go.gale.com/ps/anonymous?id=GALE%7CA107201216&sid=googleScholar&v=2.1&it=r&linkaccess=abs&issn=15254283&p=AONE&sw=w.

[7] Nakazawa, *Childhood Disrupted,* 15.

throw on my sneakers, and go for a run.

I understood that I was dealing with stress hormones, but I had no idea what to do or how to reduce the adrenaline. At the time, running or riding my mountain bike hard seemed to be the only thing that helped. Later, I learned that excessive exercise can often add to the adverse effects of stress on the nervous system. During those moments though, I couldn't stand being in my own skin.

I was consuming antacids at an excessive rate. My digestive tract was shutting down. It reached the point where I was not going to the bathroom for three or four days at a time, and eventually, it did not happen without the aid of laxatives. My skin began to itch so badly that at times I had welts over most of my body. My dermatologist put me on daily antihistamine.

In October 2017 I made an appointment with a cardiologist at the Mayo Clinic in Jacksonville, Florida. Over the following couple of months, I saw a cardiologist, a gastroenterologist, an internist, and a neurologist. I was poked and prodded and had X-rays, a sonogram, a CT scan, blood tests, cameras run down my throat, through my stomach, and into my small intestine. When they were through with that, they went in from the other end, and finally, I went through a battery of neurological tests.

It was determined that my heart was free from arteriosclerosis or narrowing of the arteries. There were no signs of any type of tumors or disease in my digestive tract or anywhere else in my body. My blood tests all came back within normal limits, other than a slightly elevated blood lipid profile.

However, they did determine I had some electrical issues. The first issue was paroxysmal atrial fibrillation, of which I was already aware. They also discovered that I had a very low HRV (heart rate variability) score and diagnosed me with cardiovagal failure,[8] which is a big word that means my vagus nerve and my heart are not communicating the way they should.

As discussed above, when you inhale your SNS signals your heart rate to increase, and when we exhale, our PSNS causes your heart to beat slower. The variation in time between heartbeats in a person with a healthy ANS should be a little different. If you look at heart rhythm as displayed on an ECG (electrocardiogram), the distance between beats to the casual observer would typically, for a healthy person, look consistent. However, because of the interaction between the SNS and the PSNS, there are slight differences between the intervals in a well-functioning nervous system. A person with a slight difference between every beat has a high HRV score.

Many athletic teams use HRV monitors to test the athletic conditioning of their athletes. The better an athlete's cardiovascular condition, the higher the score. Doctors and athletes have learned something interesting through the use of HRV monitoring. Training harder is not always the answer. The body needs rest. Training too hard can actually be detrimental to cardiovascular health. Days of rest are just as important as days of pushing the body. Too much adrenaline can adversely affect the nervous system regardless of whether it is released because of mental stress or excessive physical stress in the form of exercise. As far as our bodies are concerned, stress is stress.[9]

My neurologist discussed the possibility of trying electrical stimulation of the vagus nerve, but after further discussion, he felt the best approach for me would be to

---

[8] Phillip A. Low, Victoria A. Tomalia, & Ki Jong Park, "Autonomic function tests: Some clinical applications," *Journal of Clinical Neurology*, January 2013, https://www.thejcn.com/DOIx.php?id=10.3988/jcn.2013.9.1.1.
[9] "Your Coach as a Stress Manager," *Elite HRV*, https://elitehrv.com/your-coach-as-a-stress-manager.

learn how to reduce stress and calm my nervous system. There are no drugs for this condition. For some, serotonin reuptake inhibitors can be effective at reducing stress. One of the most well-known of these types of medications is Prozac. For me, this was not an option. Serotonin uptake inhibitors can trigger atrial fibrillation and increase the severity.

When I asked the doctor if there is a chance of reversing my situation, he said that some people get worse, and some people get better. If I did nothing to change my lifestyle and mental health, the chances were that my condition would deteriorate. If I could learn how to calm my nervous system, there was a chance that my condition would improve.

I am not alone with my nervous system issues. Manufacturers of antacids spend millions of dollars every year competing for their share of the profits driven by our nation's need for relief from heartburn. How about the countless ads on television and the internet for AFib medication and blood thinners? An even more telling sign of our cultural epidemic of stress is the multi-billion-dollar a year anti-anxiety, antidepressant, and antipsychotic pharmaceutical industry. We are a culture that has all too willingly accepted stress and being over-medicated as a normal part of life.

Dysautonomia, a term that is still unknown by most, is gaining understanding as it is related to many psychological and physical conditions. Dysautonomia is a big word used to describe a wide range of disorders and symptoms associated with autonomic nervous system disruption. Autonomic nervous system disruption as associated with PTSD falls under the umbrella of dysautonomia.

So, how does traumatic stress physically change our bodies? The key to understanding what has changed, or how this disruption occurs (dysautonomia), is to understand how our brains work. Within our brains is an area called the limbic region or limbic system. This area of the brain is made up of a complex network of systems responsible for our ability to reason, our fight-or-flight response, and our sense of well-being. The door to the limbic area is called the thalamus. This is the region of the brain that takes in information about the outside world through our sensory organs, such as the eyes, nose, ears, and skin. The thalamus then sends this information in two directions. The first to receive the information is the amygdala.

When the amygdala perceives danger, it sends a signal to the hypothalamus, which is located in the brainstem that, in turn, releases stress hormones into the body, so we are able to respond appropriately. The second area to receive the information is the hippocampus, which sends processed information to the medial prefrontal cortex, which is the portion of the brain that is responsible for reason. The hippocampus also stores memories that help us process new information. Is the perceived threat real or a false alarm? In a normally functioning brain, if the threat is perceived as a false alarm, a message is sent to stand down, and the amygdala responds by stopping the flow of hormones through the hypothalamus.

The amygdala does not understand what the threat is or why it is happening. It doesn't care—It does its job without trepidation. The danger alarm is pulled, a message is sent to the hypothalamus, stress hormones are released, the hair stands up on your arms, and you are propelled into motion. This all happens before the medial frontal cortex is able to respond. In a normally functioning brain, this isn't much of an issue. The lag in time is mere seconds.[10] The problem with someone whose brain has been conditioned by traumatic stress is that the

---

[10] van der Kolk, *The Body Keeps Score,* 60–65.

switch between the rational brain (the medial prefrontal cortex), and the automatic response system (the amygdala) gets stuck. Donna Jackson Nakazawa explains further.

> The problem is, when you are facing a lot of chronic stress, the stress response never shuts off. You're caught, perpetually, in the first half of the stress cycle. There is no state of recovery. Instead, the stress response is always mildly on—pumping out a chronic low dose of inflammatory chemicals. The stress glands—the hypothalamus, the HPA axis—secrete low levels of stress hormones all the time, leading to chronic cytokine activity and inflammation.
>
> In simplest terms: chronic stress leads to a dysregulation of our stress hormones—which leads to unregulated inflammation. And inflammation translates into symptoms and disease.[11]

The rational mind (the medial prefrontal cortex) can be completely at ease with a situation while the automatic response (the amygdala) system is on full tilt, signaling the hypothalamus to keep dumping stress hormones. After being exposed to enough traumatic stress, the switch never completely closes.[12]

The amygdala does not understand if the perceived threat is actually happening or just a memory. This is why PTSD can ensue after just one traumatic event. The amygdala of a child who has been abused does not know the difference between when the event happened and what is just a memory.

Why do some people seem to be fine after a traumatic

---

[11] Nakazawa, *Childhood Disrupted*, 30.
[12] van der Kolk, *The Body Keeps Score*, 39–43.

event while others suffer from PTSD? It is believed that the effects of PTSD can be alleviated or even avoided if one is surrounded by a loving and nurturing environment or if grief counseling begins soon after a traumatic event. Those who are able to reach a place of perceived safety with the understanding the threat is over have a much better chance of recovery and avoiding long-term health issues.[13]

This communication glitch in the limbic system is a silent killer. Most childhood sexual abuse survivors learn to live while immersed in stress hormones. In simple terms, we don't understand what it's like to live life without the constant feeling of anxiety—it becomes our normal. For many of us, when we lose that feeling we become uncomfortable—the edge is gone, and we feel like fish out of water. The problem is that many of us live for decades in this state before our bodies start breaking down, and we start experiencing physical symptoms in response to something that may have occurred twenty or thirty years before.

When neurological and autoimmune disorders first appear with minor symptoms, they are seldom associated with trauma (PTSD). Years can go by as the symptoms grow worse and increase in number before the connection is made. I am speaking from firsthand experience. By then the damage is done and the best that many can hope to achieve is to manage life in a chronic state of discomfort. For far too many people the connection between something that happened in childhood and sickness as an adult is never made.

Adverse childhood experiences (ACEs) have long-reaching health consequences. I discuss the science of adverse childhood experiences in further detail in chapter eight. Children living in adverse conditions have little

---

[13] Ibid., 51.

hope of experiencing a sense of safety or understanding that the danger is over. For many children, the threat doesn't end for years. Try telling a child whose father comes home after drinking and beats him night after night that everything is going to be OK. What about a child who lives through the contentious divorce of his or her parents? All too often children growing up in such environments lose all sense of security.

We primarily remember the events of our lives having a beginning, middle, and end. For example, remembering a trip to the beach with a friend. We remember it was a Saturday morning and that the friend picked us up in his or her car (the beginning). We arrived at the beach and spent the day swimming and lying in the sun (the middle). That afternoon we drive home (the end). It is the memory of a good day. Most of life's memories are stored in our minds in the same way.

I was first introduced to the idea that our memories are typically stored with a narrative that has a beginning, a middle, and end in Dr. Bassel van der Kolk's book, *The Body Keeps Score: Brain, Mind, and Body in the Healing of Trauma*. Dr. van der Kolk explains how trauma disrupts these memories.

> Breakdown of the thalamus explains why trauma is primarily remembered not as a story, a narrative with a beginning, middle, and end, but as isolated sensory imprints: images, sounds, and physical sensations that are accompanied by intense emotions, usually terror and helplessness.[14]

When our memories fall outside of this rhythm, we are often left in a perpetual state reliving the narrative of

---

[14] Ibid., 70.

trauma in our minds. What of a soldier who goes off to war? Many soldiers enter battle (the beginning), and a scene unfolds before their eyes for which they were unprepared (the middle). A friend dies at their side, a roadside bomb mutilates their leg, or worse. Where is the end? For some, it never ends. Every time they close their eyes, they see the event. They struggle for even a few minutes of sleep, only to be awakened in a cold sweat with the event as close as the day it happened.

This is why many of us have a hard time letting go of the past. Without understanding of what is happening, many who suffer with PTSD spend inordinate amounts of time trying to rewrite these broken narratives in their minds. This can often explain some of the seemingly inappropriate responses to everyday life experiences exhibited by those who have experienced trauma.

What of a young boy who is molested by a man, perhaps, someone they trusted, as is often the case? The memories might have a beginning and a middle, but as to an end, it is difficult to feel that something has ended if you're not sure what happened.

How many young women prepare for a date with anticipation of a romantic evening? Her heart beats with anticipation as the doorbell rings, and she is escorted to the car by someone who she believes has the same expectations (the beginning). They go dinner at a nice restaurant and have a few drinks (the middle). On the way home, they pull into a secluded spot, and he takes something from her that she was no way ready or willing to give. Where is the end? What memories is she left with? [15]

As I am writing this, my heart is beginning to pound, and the muscles in my abdomen are tightening. My amygdala is sending signals to my hypothalamus, and it is doing its job by pumping stress hormones into my body.

---

[15] Ibid.

As I am typing, as would be expected, I am thinking back at the events in my own life that have no end. The amygdala does not know the difference between the real event and a memory. I have dealt with this scenario for most of my life, even as a young child. The difference between when I was a child and now is that now I understand what is happening and can take measures before the situation spirals out of control.

As a child and even as a young adult, I suffered from extreme anxiety and depression. Often, I had no idea why. Once I began to understand how our minds work, I was able to recognize triggers that would set me into an anxious or upset state. Some of the triggers seemed to have no understandable correlation to my past. For example, the tone of someone's voice, the way someone approached me, or an off-color comment. Our subconscious minds remember things that our conscious minds have stuffed away in a dark corner.

The worst was watching the news. I never knew when a particular story would send me into a tailspin. At times I could identify the issue because I wouldn't be able to get it out of my head, sometimes for days. This is the stuff of dissociation, fragmented memories and feelings lurking just beneath the surface of our consciousness waiting to be rediscovered, often at unexpected times and often completely out of context and misunderstood.

We will revisit how this change in our minds affects our physical health in another way in chapter ten, "Sexual Dysfunction."

Chapter 5

Hypervigilance

> After a traumatic experience, the human system of self-preservation seems to go onto permanent alert, as if the danger might return at any moment.
>
> —Judith Lewis Herman, *Trauma and Recovery: The Aftermath of Violence—From Domestic Abuse to Political Terror*

Recently, I stumbled upon a Facebook post that helped me to understand that I still have some work to do. It was a typical meme with a split image. The image on top was a tranquil scene of women sitting on the edge of a cliff in the mountains taking in the scenery. The image below was a line of soldiers marching single file in full combat gear, including assault-style rifles. The meme read, "It is impossible to hike and be in a bad mood at the same time." I had a visceral response to the post. My response was not anger but deep grief and sadness. I immediately responded with the comment, "I don't think a whole lot of thought went into this post. I am sure there are families of veterans who would not agree."

I soon received comments that I was overreacting, that there was nothing wrong with the post, and that I was trying to cause a problem where there was none. My initial inclination was to defend my point of view, but out of frustration, I responded with, "If I need to explain my comment, it is unlikely you will understand." I will be the first to admit that my response was juvenile. I continued to receive pushback, and I finally deleted my comments.

I was upset. The post triggered images of young men and women marching into battle and being killed. I was astonished that the people responding to my comment didn't understand why I was upset. After I deleted my comment, I figured I would stop receiving notifications every time someone commented on the post, but they kept coming. A few other comments aired distaste for the post, but the vast majority were by veterans who viewed the post in a positive light. The next morning I was amazed at the number of veterans who responded with memories of hiking in full gear for miles or simply posted their unit's signification. It was like Old Home Week. The post seemed to draw people together in a positive way.

I am an Air Force veteran, but I have never experienced anything close to combat other than medical readiness training. After I moved past my knee-jerk response, I was somewhat happy for the people who enjoyed the post. It was great to see the camaraderie, but why did this post affect me so differently?

This post did not just brush up against an ingrained sensibility; it pulled a significant trigger. I was manifesting symptoms of anxiety that I had not displayed for months. The following morning I experienced a significant episode of disassociation. I "checked out." As discussed earlier, when I am coming out of this state I often have no idea where I am or what I'm doing and very often am not cognizant of myself. It doesn't last long—typically five or ten seconds—but it is very unsettling, to say the least. This time was especially discouraging because it had been almost a year since my last episode. I had hoped I had worked through the issue. Later in the day, I began having heart palpitations, which by that evening manifested as full-blown atrial fibrillation.

Why was I affected in such a way? The debilitating issue with those of us who suffer from PTSD is our past. Yes, the memories of our past are troubling and cause significant stress, remorse, and fear, but the overarching issue is caused by the events of our past, not the memories themselves.

Let me explain further. The average person starts out encapsulated in a protective shell of security. This shell is a place of safety and provides a sense of well-being. This shell is slowly worn away over time as we experience life bit by bit within the care of a loving family or community. Most well-adjusted people do not completely shed the shell until they are well into their thirties or even later in life. Some never lose the shell.

What happens when that shell is ripped away or shattered? What if a child grows up with no memory of the shell whatsoever? Consider a child who goes off to war. Most of the young men who we send into battle have no idea what they are about to face, and are little more than children.

If all goes well, children are nurtured with the understanding that their mother and father will care for them. They are raised in the security of their mother's arms without a thought that harm could come to them if they remain within reach. Many children in our culture are raised with the understanding of a benevolent God who sits in Heaven and cares for His children.

What happens when that child steps onto the battlefield, shots are fired in their direction, and the world is exploding in chaos all around them? Many of them cry out to their benevolent God. Some clutch their rosaries, given to them by their mothers for protection as they witness the unthinkable. In mere moments, several of these young men go from believing that justice will prevail to frantically trying to hold on to their very lives or the broken pieces of their friends' bodies. The shell of their security is ripped away and shattered before they have any idea of what has happened. Everything they believed about life being fair, safe, and just is brutally destroyed in the blink of an eye.

Flags of Our Fathers, written by James Bradley and Ron Powers, is a heart-gripping book honoring the lives and service of the six Iwo Jima flag raisers. James Bradley is the son of John Bradley, a Navy corpsman who administered aid to Easy Company of the 2nd Battalion, 28th Marines, and 5th Marine Division as they fought for the island of Iwo Jima—one of the most horrifying battles of World War II. The following words need no further commentary.

> All their young lives their heads had been filled by military propaganda, in grade school, high school, and now in the army. Since their youth they had been told how true Japanese heroes always "died with the Emperor's name on their lips." Death on the battlefield was glorified for the home front, but the veterans knew that the last word of a boy dying in battle was someone else's name, not the Emperor's. It was the same name all troops throughout history had cried out with their last breath. It was rendered in different tongues, but the meaning was universal. His last word was invariably "Okason!" The German would cry "Mutter!" The English and Americans, "Mother!" "Mom!" or "Mommy!"[1]

I shrink with trepidation to include the trauma that I have experienced with those who have lived through the horrors of war. I cannot even begin to conceive what those men went through on the island of Iwo Jima in 1945, but I have no doubt that it was as close to hell as one could experience during this life.

---

[1] James Bradley & Ron Powers, *Flags of our Fathers* (New York: Bantam, 2000), 137.

When we live through traumatic events that shatter our false shell of security, it changes the way we view the world. For many of us, the change is somewhat immediate. For others it happens through the slow, mind-numbing abuse suffered by so many children. So often it changes not only the way we view the world but also our core perception of security. It changes the way we view family and friends, our social structure, our country, and yes, even God. Regardless of how much we try to convince ourselves that we trust, our understanding of the world around us has changed.

The Merriam-Webster Dictionary defines hypervigilance as "extreme or excessive vigilance: the state of being highly or abnormally alert to potential danger or threat." Hypervigilance is often accompanied by a state of hyperarousal, the inability to relax—typically associated with fight of flight or hypoarousal,[2] the state of becoming numb to our emotions. These two sides of the same coin are often associated with combat veterans who overreact to loud or sudden noises or flashbacks. They are either driven into state of seemingly irrational panic or become numb and go off into a catatonic sate.[3] Children who have been sexually or physically abused live in a heightened state of alertness, looking for the bogeyman around every corner. Every person they meet could become the bogeyman at any moment. A teacher, pastor, lifelong friend, spouse, or parent could come under suspicion. As I look back at my own life, I seemed to drift back and forth between the states of hyperarousal and hypoarousal. Based on my own observations and the stories I have read, this may be the case with most people who have experienced abuse.

---

[2] Aundi Kolber, *Try Softer: A Fresh Approach to Move Us out of Anxiety, Stress, and Survival Mode—And into a Life of Connection and Joy* (Tyndale, 2020), 32.
[3] Bessel van der Kolk, *The Body Keeps the Score: Brain, Mind, and Body in the Healing of Trauma* (New Your, NY: Penguin, 2015), 23.

Bessel van der Kolk describes what happened when he and his colleagues decided to show a group of children who had suffered abuse a group of everyday images that they cut out of magazines.

> The responses of the clinic children were alarming. The most innocent images stirred up intense feelings of danger, aggression, sexual arousal, and terror. We had not selected these photos because they had some hidden meaning that sensitive people could uncover; they were ordinary images of everyday life. We could only conclude that for abused children, the whole world is filled with triggers. As long as they can imagine only disastrous outcomes to relatively benign situations, anybody walking into a room, any stranger, any image, on a screen or on a billboard might be perceived as a harbinger of catastrophe. In this light the bizarre behavior of the kids at the children's clinic made perfect sense.[4]

Trust and feeling secure for abused children is not just difficult; for many it is entirely outside the realm of possibility. Many reading this book will relate to the little feeling of trepidation every time we greet somebody, even family members or close friends, always wondering what that person thinks of us or what they may be planning to do to us.

Many of us can become incensed, offended, or hurt over the most benign and innocent comments or actions of others. Even as adults, many of us have difficulty with social interaction—sabotaging relationships over the silliest things that most people wouldn't give a second thought.

---

[4] van der Kolk, *The Body Keeps Score*, 110.

Years ago I was part of a group at church for men dealing with addiction issues. During one of the meetings, a man (who is also a friend of mine) told a story about a situation he encountered. As he told his story, he was being self-deprecating and chuckling to break the tension. After he was through speaking, I said, "What an idiot." Thinking back on the situation, I realize that my comment was completely inappropriate, but at the time it was meant as lighthearted agreement—laughing along with him. Growing up, calling someone an idiot was often used as light, playful banter between friends.

When I made my comment, I did not detect any negative reaction from my friend, and the group conversation continued as usual. However, about a week after the meeting, I received a phone call from the friend who I called an idiot. From the word "Hello," I had no doubt that he was furious with me and very hurt because of my flippant comment. This guy was my friend, and nothing in me felt he was an idiot. He spent a week feeling hurt and upset because of a passing comment I made and never thought about again—that is, until I received his phone call. This happened over twenty years ago, but I have never forgotten it since.

I could relate all too well to what my friend was feeling. The reason the situation was so impactful to me is that I have stood in his shoes, countless times. I have spent days, weeks, and even years obsessing about what someone thinks about me because of a foolish comment. More times than not, my obsessive worrying turns into resentment and anger. Over what? A comment or incident that someone else never gave a second thought.

I have spent days locked in this cycle of obsessive worrying over someone not returning a phone call—worrying about what I may have said or done—playing my most recent interactions with that person over and over again in my head. I would spend an entire weekend with my stomach in a knot only to receive a phone call on Monday—"Hey, man, sorry I didn't call you before now. I had a crazy day on Friday and went out of town with the family this weekend. What's going on?"

Children who suffer the trauma of abuse become hypervigilant as a mode of survival. It is not an instinct but learned behavior. The mind becomes conditioned to be on a constant lookout for the bogeyman in every person they encounter. Many children who have been abused wake up every morning with stress hormones flooding through their system, ready and waiting for the next assault. It becomes a way of life—the normal of their existence.

Many trauma survivors who are prescribed drugs to help reduce stress, anxiety, or depression complain that they don't like how the medication makes them feel. This feeling is often called "emotional blunting." A common complaint is that they feel they're "losing their edge."[5]. I can relate, all too well. We become accustomed to life being amped-up on stress hormones, and when that goes away, we don't know how to function.

I was well into adulthood before I realized I had no idea how to relax. During my recovery process, I began practicing mediation and doing stretching exercises to help my body relax. It was during this process, in my late forties, that I discovered that I carry stress in my abdomen. I had no idea how to do something as simple as allow my abdominal muscles to relax.

My place of refuge has always been in nature. I often refer to the woods as the cathedral of the forest. Being in the woods and away from people is where I feel closest to God and at peace. Years ago I went for a weekend backpacking excursion. The state forest that I chose for my

---

[5] Bid, 227.

getaway had designated campsites along the trails. Once I settled into my site, and the sun went down, I made a fire, ate dinner, and called Mary on my cell phone.

During our call, she could hear a group of coyotes howling a hundred yards or so from my campsite. She asked if I was nervous about coyotes being in the area. I wasn't worried at all about the coyotes and enjoyed the sound of them howling. Between them and the little foxes, they had quite a chorus going on at times. My answer to her was, "No, not at all, but what I am concerned about is the group of hikers camping at the next site over."

When people become our source of stress, the world becomes a difficult place to navigate. Abused children develop hypervigilance as a defense mechanism—the constant fear of being harmed develops into a vow never to allow themselves to be hurt under any circumstance. This vow is seldom spoken or even consciously considered, but it develops just the same, indelibly programmed into the subconscious mind because people—all people—have proven untrustworthy or even dangerous. This vow manifests itself in the faces of children in different ways. Some become terribly introverted and incurably shy while keeping the world at arm's length, some become seemingly disorganized, having a difficult time staying on task with rambunctious and very often irrational outbursts (ADHD), and others become defiant and angry, with an attitude of, "Back off, I can do this myself. Just leave me alone." These are the faces of freighted and very often terribly misunderstood children regardless of how they appear to the world. At times they display a combination of these types of behaviors—children who many parents and most school systems have no idea how to deal with.

As these children grow into adults, these vows become much more ingrained. In chapter four I discussed how our memories have a beginning, middle, and end. As we grow past childhood, so much of our lives become about rewriting the narrative of our past—proving to ourselves and the world that we are in control. Inordinate amounts of our time become about rewriting all the endings. Many of us are completely unaware of what we are doing or why. We may become aware of the crazy cycle that has taken control of our lives, but far too many of us have no idea why we are doing it, when it started, or how to stop.

The mental health community has a name for this crazy cycle: codependency. Some people reading this may be wondering how hypervigilance could be tied to codependency, a condition typically associated with a dysfunctional relationship with an addict, also referred to as a dependent. This is something I wondered when my therapist handed me a book titled *Codependency No More* by Melody Beattie. I will discuss this book and codependency as it relates to child abuse survivors in the next chapter. This is another one of those things that wish I had learned about many years ago.

Chapter 6

Codependency

We can't be so desperate for love that we forget where we can always find it; within.

— Alexandra Elle

I had heard the term codependency for many years without having any real idea of the implications. I associated the condition with the manipulative and controlling behavior that develops in a person as a result of living with an alcoholic or drug addict (a dependent), which is how the condition, for the most part, was originally identified. Perhaps this condition should be called "adaptation," or "survival mode." Nobody should ever have to live with someone who abuses drugs or alcohol. Most normal, healthy people will become manipulative and controlling when caught up in such an environment. When a person lives with an abusive drunk, who is the one who suffers?

As the mental health profession began to accept codependency as a valid condition, they also started to recognize that its effects are farther reaching than initially understood. They have discovered that many more people other than just the dependents of alcoholics and drug addicts are affected. To explain further, the following is an excerpt from the book Codependent No More by Melody Beattie.

> However, the definition for codependency has expanded since then. Professionals began to better understand the effects of the chemically dependent person on the family, and the effects

of the family on the chemically dependent person. Professionals began to identify other problems such as overeating and undereating, gambling, and certain sexual behaviors. These compulsive disorders paralleled the compulsive disorder, or illness, of alcoholism. Professionals also began to notice many people in close relationships with these compulsive people developed patterns of reacting and coping that resembled the coping patterns of people in relationships with alcoholics. Something peculiar had happened to these families, too.

As professionals began to understand codependency better, more groups of people appeared to have it: adult children of alcoholics; people in relationships with emotionally or mentally disturbed persons; people in relationships with chronically ill people; parents of children with behavior problems; people in relationships with irresponsible people; professionals— nurses, social workers, and others in "helping" occupations. Even recovering alcoholics and addicts noticed they were codependent and perhaps had been long before becoming chemically dependent. Codependents started cropping up everywhere.[1]

As I read Beattie's book, I was confused as to the source of my codependent behavior. I have never spent time enabling, covering for, or repeatedly rescuing an addict. Sure, I have been around my fair share of dysfunction, and codependency seemed like a family trait, but I still had a hard time seeing how I fit the mold.

It wasn't until I began to understand the idea of "res-

---

[1] Melody Beattie, *Codependent No More: How to Stop Controlling Others and Start Caring for Yourself* (New York: Harper & Row, 1987), 30.

cuing" as it applies to codependency that I realized I fit the mold quite well. The definition implies more than just helping someone escape a situation of need, danger, or impending doom. The rescue of the codependent develops from our need to be rescued. From what? The answer is not so simple: grief, loneliness, the feeling that we have no value, the belief that we are somehow fatally flawed or broken.

Codependency doesn't always start this way. Many people become beaten down as a result of living with and caring for an abusive addict. Others are beaten or abused as children. Far too many children in this world never have a chance. From as early as they can remember, they are told through the words and actions of their abusers that they are worthless—that they are not like everyone else, and they don't deserve the good things of life because they are stupid.

Many of us feel the need to be rescued from our abyss of loneliness and self-hatred. We live under the false belief that if we can just prove our value to another, we will receive the love we so desperately desire. Perhaps we may even find someone who will help us become something of value. As this belief takes hold, we begin to rescue others. We most likely have no understanding of what we are doing when we begin. We merely think, *What if I can just be a hero to somebody?* We just want to hear simple words like, "You did a great job," "Thank you," or "That was just what I needed." If someone would just give us an approving nod or a word of kindness, we would give that person anything.

I didn't just rescue people who I felt needed to be rescued. I tried rescuing everybody. I helped people who never asked for or needed my help. I took responsibility for and worried about everything and everybody.

Here's more from Beattie on this.

Whether codependents appear fragile and helpless, or sturdy and powerful, most of us are frightened, needy, vulnerable children who are aching and desperate to be loved and cared for.

This child in us believes we are unlovable and will never find the comfort we are seeking; sometimes this vulnerable child becomes too desperate. People have

abandoned us, emotionally and physically. People have rejected us. People have abused us, let us down. People have never been there for us; they have not seen, heard, or responded to our needs. We may come to believe that people will never be there for us. For many of us, even God seems to have gone away.

We have been there for so many people. Most of us desperately want someone to finally be there for us. We need someone, anyone, to rescue us from the stark loneliness, alienation, and pain. We want some of the good stuff, and the good stuff is not in us. Pain is in us. We feel so helpless and uncertain. Others look so powerful and assured. We conclude the magic must be in them.

So we become dependent on them. We can become dependent on lovers, spouses, friends, parents, or our children. We become dependent on their approval. We become dependent on their presence. We become dependent on their need for us. We become dependent on their love, even though we believe we will never receive their love; we believe we are unlovable and nobody has ever loved us in a way that met our needs.[2]

I have spent so much of my life feeling as though others had "the good stuff." When I was a teenager, far too often my emotions hinged on my need for affirmation from my friends, and I hated being alone. I'm not sure I ever considered that fact so many years ago. As I look back, I realize I didn't know how to be alone. Teenagers, by their very nature, are social creatures, but I took things to the extreme. If one friend couldn't hang out, I would call another. If none of my friends could hang out, I would go downtown, hang out in a bar, or hitchhike somewhere—anywhere other than where I was.

I grew up in a small town on the coast of Connecticut. More than once I found myself sobering up in New York City. I needed to be around people. Coming to in the early hours of the morning on a subway in Harlem is an experience not easily forgotten—and a story for another time. A word of advice: if you ever find yourself drunk and hitchhiking on Interstate 95 in the middle of the night, it is way easier hitching a ride into Manhattan than it is getting out. Every lonely drunk headed into the city will be glad to give you a ride. Unless you have a pocket full of cash, good luck escaping. I never had any money. That's what happens when you get hammered and hitchhike into New York City—you wake up broke.

As I grew older, got married, started working, and settled somewhat into my role as an adult, my incessant need for affirmation and my discomfort with being alone continued. Here is the thing about being addicted to affirmation: it is not so easily identified. It's not like being addicted to alcohol or other substances. When you get drunk and do something stupid, the reason for your stupidity is most often easily identified.

---

[2] Ibid., 90.

Most can relate to, "Hey man, I'm sorry for what I did. I was really drunk and didn't know what I was doing." What do we say to someone who we have hurt because of our manipulation? "Sorry man, I know I was a complete jerk. I have this problem with low self-esteem, so I get a little creepy sometimes." For the most part, neither we nor the people we are attempting to attach ourselves to have any idea what is happening. It was quite some time into my recovery and getting to know myself before I was able to recognize and admit to my behavior.

Most well-adjusted people have little desire or tolerance for maintaining relationships with controlling, manipulative, and needy people, so codependent people find it difficult to form healthy relationships. Most often we find ourselves surrounded by dependents, which does nothing more than feed our codependency. The tempo of our lives becomes a cycle of frustration and dysfunction.

Codependency is a cycle. As codependents, many of us view ourselves as the responsible ones. We take responsibility for everything and everyone. The underlying reason we do this is that our sense of value and self-worth hinges on other people's opinions of us—the very essence of codependency. Most of us give in to and worry about others until we are exhausted. Once we are exhausted, we become resentful.

Why shouldn't we be resentful? We give and give and never feel like anyone ever considers our needs. At times we even blow up and display our resentment. We are the ones who give meaning to the words passive-aggressive. Once we finally express ourselves, we feel guilty that we have hurt somebody's feelings (the dependent) and go to extraordinary lengths to make amends. We stuff down our own needs and apologize to someone when we have done nothing wrong. The codependent life becomes about approval—becoming the man or woman who everyone needs. It is irrational, and yet we pursue it at any cost.[3]

Many of us spend our days visiting or calling people we perceive as our friends, "Hey, I was thinking of you and wanted to see how you are doing." Many mornings would start with wondering who I could take to lunch because I needed companionship. There is nothing wrong with developing friendships and needing companionship. It is a healthy human need, but we need to check our motivation. Are we calling to inquire if someone can go to lunch because we desire to spend time with a particular individual, or will anyone do? If Johnny isn't available, do we call Fred? And if Fred isn't available, do we call Jimmy? You see where I'm going with this. Churches are a great place for affirmation addicts to seek fulfillment. Churches are like a magnet for controlling, manipulative, and needy people. That's why people are there—to be rescued and to rescue. This subject could be another book all in itself.

One of my counselors explained a universal rule to me: codependents attract dependents like steel shavings to a magnet. Codependents enter relationships, intentionally or not, that are controlling, manipulative, and needy. Dependents pick up on this vibe. Most do this instinctively without giving it a second thought, and within no time they are using the codependent's controlling behavior to control the codependent. It is a dance that has been going on since the beginning of time, a self-perpetuating cycle. The codependent is happy with the arrangement because he or she feels his or her needs are getting met while the dependent slowly sucks the life out of the codependent.

How do we stop this cycle? The answer is simple: we disconnect. Not in anger, we simply stop reaching out. I strongly suggest that you do not even think of doing this unless you are seeing a mental health counselor regularly.

---

[3] Ibid., 30.

Why? Because it's going to hurt! I disconnected while I was seeing a counselor, and as much as I hate to admit it, I spent many lonely nights at home driven deeper into my addictions.

This was when I learned that coffee shops are great places to be when we don't want to be alone while at the same time we don't feel like talking to people. Movie theaters are another great place. There was a period of time when I saw every movie released, some of them multiple times. I was terrified to be alone. It was time to face my emotions and the reality that I needed to change. I was forty-three years old, and as cliché as it may sound, I had no idea who I was. All I knew is that I was the worst, most broken, dysfunctional individual that I knew. The thought of spending time alone scared the crap out of me.

I did most of this "getting to know myself" while living alone in the mountains of North Carolina. For most of my life, I have dreamed about spending time alone in the mountains. The fantasy was nothing like the reality. The silence and loneliness became painful beyond what I could have ever dreamed or imagined.

In literature and the movies, someone who is banished to isolation for his or her crimes is, as an act of mercy, given a gun with one bullet. That bullet is a way of escape when the assault of that person's demons becomes more than he or she can bear. There were times when I would get up in the middle of the night, get in my car, and drive anywhere to escape the noise in my head.

For the most part, my phone remained silent. Months went by, and the few people who did call wanted something from me. The call would typically start with, "Hey, man, I just called to see how you are doing," and within a very short period of time would segue into, "Oh, by the way, while I have you on the phone . . ." They had little interest in how I was doing—they needed something. You can tell when you have disconnected yourself from a dependent. They often get resentful, antagonistic, or sarcastic as a last-ditch effort to continue the dance.

The problem of not approving of ourselves, self-loathing, or self-hatred is that these emotions often do not display themselves on the surface of our understanding. The belief that we are somehow broken or not worth as much as other people can reside deep within our subconscious minds. These assumptions about ourselves become so deeply seated and ingrained that we act on them without understanding what we are doing. The idea that I was broken and not the same as others was reaffirmed continuously throughout my childhood.

My parents and my teachers repeatedly reminded me that I had a learning disability. I was labeled as a retard and heard that said to me in one way or another several times a day until I was halfway through high school. I was bullied relentlessly for years. It's no wonder I twitched uncontrollably, but that does not mean I am broken. I may be wounded, but I can heal. I may have been sexually and physically abused and made to feel that I had no control over my body or my circumstances, but once again, that does not mean I am broken. It does mean, however, that I needed time to heal.

One of the most difficult things about healing from codependency is coming to an understanding of where to reach out for help. Where do we start? As codependents, once we understand that we need to heal, we most often reach out to other people who we feel "have it all together." We have spent so much of our lives feeling completely inadequate that we look toward others who appear to have all the answers. For example, we may look toward a pastor or a family member to solve our problems. If the people we are looking to rescue us refuse to help or can't help, we feel rejected or angry. We constantly set ourselves up for rejection and anger because we don't understand that other people couldn't fix our problems even if they wanted to do so.

The first thing that we must get through our heads is that we shouldn't be trying to control other people, and other people are not responsible for our well-being. We are only responsible for ourselves. Other people are not responsible for our happiness, sadness, joy, or grief. Other people can't make us happy or sad. Other people can't make us mad. We get mad, glad, or sad because of the way we chose to respond to any given situation.

I stumbled across an interview with singer-songwriter Jewel in *Mindful* magazine called "In Search of Wholeness." I was deeply touched by what Jewel had to say.

> At one point, she (Jewel) tells me, she had a realization. "What if I am not broken? What if I shouldn't approach this from the concept that I 'm broken and I need to be fixed? That's a horrible proposition to start from, because you are saying that the answer is outside myself, healing is outside myself. So I decided to tackle it from the idea that, what if I exist perfectly at all times? And it's really just a matter of doing an archeological dig back into my real self?
>
> "That's where the work of creating happiness begins," she says: "digging through the mud and gunk that life heaps on, unwinding habits you develop out of necessity that no longer serve you, and to examine the thoughts that run your mind, to see if they reflect the truth."[4]

Let's say you are finally convinced that you need to

---

[4] Kellie Walsh, "Singer-Songwriter Jewel Shares Her Mindfulness Practices," *Mindful.org*, October 20, 2017, https://www.mindful.org/singer-jewel-shares-mindfulness-practices.

stop looking to others for healing; where do you start? You start within! For most people, it is a slow, painful process, but as time goes by, it becomes rewarding and even enjoyable. It's fine to seek the help of a mental health professional, but keep in mind that this person cannot fix your problems. A counselor can help guide you in the right direction, but a counselor is not your healer. Recovery can be exciting and fun when you discover the real you that is waiting to emerge into a brand-new life. This may sound like another cliché, but it is very true.

I am not a healthcare professional; I am simply a person who wants to share my story and experiences so that you might have the opportunity to glean something from my life as I have from others. What I have written in this chapter, and in this book as a whole, only begins to cover the implications and effects of codependency. I understand that I have covered quite a bit of ground, and it is a considerable amount of information to take all at once. I suggest that in addition to counseling you pick up a copy of *Codependent No More* by Melody Beattie. Her insights have been an instrumental part of my recovery.

I have heard it said that we are all codependent, and in some regards, that is true in that our capacity for compassion is a God-given attribute. We are to love our neighbors as we love ourselves (Matthew 12:31). This is the second-greatest commandment, but when compassion turns into control or bondage, it is no longer healthy or the way that God intended for us to live.

Let me assure you that the road to recovery is worth every bump and bruise that we suffer along the way. I admit I have allowed the pendulum to swing a little too far in the opposite direction. I have now become a bit of a loner, keeping people at arm's length, being far too suspicious of their motives. For my next act, I need to allow the pendulum to swing back in the other direction. We are all a work in progress; the key is to keep moving forward.

I am so thankful for my family, who has stuck by my side through thick and thin. It is important to me to let them know how much I love them. I tell them as often as possible and they respond in kind—whenever we hang up the phone or part for a time—which has become the habit between all of our family members. But, when I dig deep and examine the intentions of my heart, I'm not so sure that my motivation isn't as much that I need to hear that I am loved. I guess I am still a little codependent, but we all are. We all need to know how much we are loved.

With all that I have been through, there are three individuals with whom I willingly continue the codependent dance. Their names are Teddy, Mattie (Madeline), and Izzy (Isabella), the three little puppies that rule our house. They are not really puppies anymore, but they always will be in my heart, kind of like my kids will always be kids. At bedtime we have a ritual to which we all look forward. They know when it's bedtime. It's amazing. If I stay up a little later than usual, I will have three little fuzz balls circling my chair, staring me down in anticipation. They want to go to bed, and they want their treat.

This ritual happens every night regardless if they left a puddle by the door, decided to destroy a pillow, or had me chasing them through the neighborhood because they don't always listen. I want them to go to bed at night, knowing they are loved, and yes, I love to see them dance around in excitement. I give them their treat and pat them on their heads and tell them what a good boy or girl they are.

We have a Father in heaven that loves us even more than I love my puppies, even when we do foolish things. Always keep the truth in your heart that God doesn't love you because of how good you are. He loves you because He is good.

I would like to end this chapter with the words to a song that I would sit and sing over and over again during my recovery—alone with just God and my guitar. I still have a hard time singing this song with a dry eye.

> Lord it is You Who created the heavens.
> Lord it is Your Hand that put the stars in their place.
> Lord it is Your Voice that commands the morning.
> Even oceans and their waves bow at Your Feet.
>
> Lord who am I compared to your glory, oh Lord.
> Lord Who am I compared to Your Majesty.
>
> I am your beloved, Your creation, and You love me as I am.
> You have called me chosen for Your Kingdom, unashamed to call me your own.
>
> I am your beloved.[5]

---

[5] Brent Helming, *Your Beloved*, 1996, Mercy/Vineyard Publishing.

Chapter 7

My Teenage Years

> In my view, suicide is not really a wish for life
> to end. "What is it then?" It is the only way a
> powerless person can find to make everybody
> else look away from his shame.
> The wish is not to die, but to hide.
>
> —Orson Scott Card, *Ender's Shadow*

I am not so sure that Orson Scott Card's statement above is true of all those who wish to leave this life, but for me, it rings with peals of truth. When my family moved to a new town, I was looking forward to leaving *me* behind, never to be heard from again. But how can we hide from ourselves? Shame had not just become an emotion; it had become an identity. Every motivation, my reasoning—every thought or idea that I had—originated and ended in shame. Shame kept me stuck in the past and stole my hope for the future.

What I am about to share is, without question, the most difficult thing I have ever expressed in words. Much of what I have written in this book about my past I have never shared with anyone other than my therapist. The reason I am saying this is because I want you to understand the struggle.

The odd thing is that although the events of my past have kept me trapped in shame, they are not what I fear. What I fear now is what I have always feared—people knowing the truth of my past—my wife, my children, people at work, and my friends. I was hemmed in, with shame closing in from behind as fear crippled my forward progress. But why? Is it that I fear people's knowledge of the abuse? It's not quite that simple. It runs much deeper.

Sharing about the abuse is the easy part. The most frightening part is allowing people into my heart. In other words, sharing my feelings. What I fear most is what life has taught me to fear: intimacy (trust). This begs the question: "Why do I have such an overwhelming need to share my story?" I will answer this question in chapter thirteen, but the short answer is that I'm tired of hiding in the shadows of my past. Deep within I think we all know that exposing every dark recess of our lives to the light is our only path to freedom.

At the end of chapter two I wrote about an older boy who had been abusing me—the boy who had gotten rough with me and slammed my foot in the door when I was trying to get away. It was a long time ago, but to the best of my memory, about a year later I called him to ask if he wanted to have sex.

I called him after I had gone through puberty. I wanted to prove to him that there was nothing wrong with me. I wanted to feel accepted. When he was rough with me and slammed my foot in the door, part of me thought he acted that way because I was unable to ejaculate. I know this thinking makes little sense at all, but very little makes sense to a confused child. When we talked on the phone, he asked me if I could "cum" (ejaculate). When I told him that I could, I thought he would be happy. I don't remember exactly what he said, but this part of the story ends with nothing happening. He was not interested, and I was left crushed and humiliated, driven deeper into confusion.

The cords of my emotions were so entangled at that point in my life that I'm sure I had no idea what I was feeling. What I do remember feeling is shame and absolute rejection.

Same-sex attraction has been a significant trigger for me for most of my life. At the sight of someone who I felt was gay, the memories of what happed would come flooding into my mind, and they still do at times. It is inescapable. Here is the problem with these associations that I had formed between what happened to me and homosexuality: they were formed in the mind of a confused and traumatized child.

I now understand that I equated homosexual acts of molestation with homosexuality or same-sex attraction. What an unfair assessment, but it was all I was capable of understanding. There are plenty of women who molest young boys, just as there are plenty of men that molest young girls. I don't believe that sexual abuse of children has to do with attraction as much as it has to do with mental illness. Don't misunderstand what I am saying—yes, there are pedophiles who seem to prey on one specific gender or the other. What I'm saying is that I don't believe the boy who molested me did it because he was attracted to me. It wasn't personal; any little boy would have satisfied his desires. Based on the evidence that I have uncovered, the record is clear that sexual abuse in not a homosexual issue any more than it is a heterosexual issue—mental illness is a human issue.

You may think my confusion concerning same-sex relationships stemmed from the social climate of the 1970s and 1980s or perhaps because of my religious convictions. There is some truth to that assessment. At that time, same-sex relationships were not as accepted as they are today. As children we used terms such as "faggot" and "queer" as insults. Homosexuality was openly ridiculed and looked down upon.

A huge part of me feels compassion for those living a homosexual lifestyle. I understand the pain, confusion, anger, and resentment that comes from being looked down on and chastised for something that others don't understand. It hurts when I hear someone speak unkindly about someone who is gay. I am not innocent in this regard, however. I have made some terrible statements about those in the gay community. For that I am truly sorry.

My hope is that one day I will be able to love people without the cloud of sexuality, a day when I won't look at people as being straight or gay, ugly or pretty, or sexually attractive—just as people.

While I acknowledge that social stigma and my religious beliefs may have been part of the issue, I don't think they were the primary reason for my confusion. The main reason for my confusion is that I am not gay. This is an issue that I struggled with as a teenager. I have never pursued a same-sex relationship, but I did spend time wondering what was happening to me. I would wake up in a panic, having had a dream about having sex with another man.[1] These are issues that have followed me in adulthood. I have fantasized about having sex with other men—something I would not want to happen. The fact that I am not alone in fantasizing about such things is of little comfort. It is not at all uncommon for men and women alike to dream about, fantasize about, or even find themselves sexually aroused at the thought of the very thing that torments them—such as rape victims fantasizing and/or obsessing about being raped. Some mental health professionals assert that such fantasies result from deep-seated fear or shame, while others claim that they occur out of a need to gain control of the past.[2]

---

[1] Bessel van der Kolk, *The Body Keeps the Score: Brain, Mind, and Body in the Healing of Trauma* (New Your, NY: Penguin, 2015), 205.
[2] David J. Ley, "The Rape Fantasy: Does the Rape Fantasy actually MEAN anything?," *Psychology Today*, December 28, 2010,
https://www.psychologytoday.com/us/blog/women-who-stray/201012/the-rape-fantasy.

I am very uncomfortable seeing a man unclothed. It is not as simple as not finding the nude image of a man unattractive; I become uncomfortable. You may wonder how someone who is uncomfortable with male nudity could be addicted to pornography. After all, pornography is full of images of naked men. I have wondered the same thing, but as I began learning about sexual addiction, the answer became clear. Sexual addiction is an issue that we will visit in chapter nine, but for now let me say that sexual abuse and pornography destroys our capacity for intimacy.

Sexual abuse is traumatic, but it is also human touch. God gave us the gift of physical union as something to be shared between two people in a romantic, intimate bond. For so many of us who have been sexually abused, our understanding of intimacy and sexuality becomes tainted. Sexuality is all too often the best we can do when it comes to fulfilling our deep God-given need for human touch. The idea of intimacy becomes overwhelming, altogether misunderstood and confusing, and all too often triggers feelings of shame and/or anger.[3]

I recently went to someone's home and there was a painting of a nude male hanging on the wall, and I had knots in my stomach and became extremely anxious. The image was tastefully done, nothing lewd or obscene, just a painting of the backside of a male figure. There was nothing sexually suggestive about the image whatsoever. Instead, it spoke of intimacy.

I often wonder if women who have been abused by men have the same feelings. Because of how my life started out, I have a hard time opening up to men. I have always responded better being counseled by women. Although I do not understand being physically attracted to the male physique, this does not mean I can't recognize

---

[3] van der Kolk, *The Body Keeps Score*, 13.

when a man is good looking. I'll be the first to admit that there are actors from different movies who I have a "man crush" on, but that doesn't mean I want to have sex with them. This may sound like a contradiction to some, but there's a huge difference between finding someone beautiful or handsome and desiring them sexually.

There was a time when I thought there was something wrong with me because I felt a man was handsome. Just the thought of it put me into a tailspin. The truth is that there is nothing wrong with finding another man good looking. I would just prefer that they not take off their clothes. I chuckled a little when I wrote that. Why do you think the advertising industry uses men in advertising campaigns for products predominantly purchased by men? This is also true for women. Most feminine products are advertised using female models. Women seem to be much more open to finding other women attractive.

As I began to look back at this situation with this older boy, it was important to begin to separate the cords of my emotions. What was I thinking when I called him? Was I looking for love? I'm not sure I understood love at that point in my life, but it would be fair to say I was looking for something to fill the hole in my heart. I wanted to be affirmed and accepted, but in my confusion, I set myself up for rejection.

The thing about sexual abuse is that it steals a part of us, leaving us empty and ashamed. I was longing for something so simple but unattainable—acceptance! Not only did I not receive that, I was mocked, belittled, and shamed—left discarded and alone. Could I have articulated my grief at the time? How can we possibly explain what we don't understand? And who was there to listen?

So, yes, I was looking for love in the only way I understood. This desperate reach for love and acceptance festered through the years and became a twisted knot of hatred, shame, guilt, and confusion.

One of the most confusing and all too often misunderstood issues that sexual abuse victims are forced to face is what I consider a dual role in the relationship. I have used the word "relationship" purposely because in many cases it is just that, a relationship. Often abuse victims forge emotional ties with their abuser. These relationships involve victims who quite often do not understand that they are victims and become facilitators of the abuse by covering for the abuser as a codependent. When this older boy was abusing me, I covered for him with my parents. As we delve deeper into these issues, it becomes clear how traumatic stress can give birth to codependency. Often the trauma inflicted on the victim, especially if inflicted over a long period, will cause a dependent/codependent relationship.

Let's return to Dr. van Der Kolk once again.

> Children are also programmed to be fundamentally loyal to their caretakers, even if they are abused by them. Terror increases the need for attachment, even if the source of comfort is also the source of terror. I have never met a child below the age of ten who was tortured at home (and who had broken bones and burned skin to show for it) who, if given the option, would not have chosen to stay with his or her family rather than being placed in a foster home. Of course, clinging to one's abuser is not exclusive to childhood. Hostages have put up bail for their captors, expressed a wish to marry them, or had sexual relations with them; victims of domestic violence often cover up for their abusers. Judges often tell me how humiliated they feel when they try to protect victims of domestic violence by issuing restraining orders, only to find out that many of them secretly al-

low their partners to return.[4]

As I mentioned in chapter two, when I was twelve my family moved to the town of Westbrook, CT. The town was so small that they combined the junior high and the high school into one: Westbrook Jr. Sr. High School. I was blessed to be enrolled in a special education program overseen by a teacher who felt I had the ability to learn in a mainstream learning atmosphere. Thank the Lord for good teachers like Mr. Bialicky. After being administered a battery of tests, they determined I would be assimilated into regular classes during my freshman year of high school. During that year, I attended regular classes while still being part of the special education program until it was determined that I was able to function within a "normal" classroom environment.

I have some great memories of high school, but I also wrestled with immature emotions and social habits. I was extremely insecure and had low self-esteem. Our high school basketball coach, Mr. Freeman, took an interest in helping me, and let me assure you, it was not because of my athletic abilities. As I have shared, I was tall and thin and pretty much a wimp. A tall wimp with low self-esteem and anger issues is not a pretty picture. Like my special education teacher, my basketball coach was one of the few teachers who cared about his students. He spent a great deal of time working with me and several other students after school on conditioning, strength training, and the fundamentals of the game. When he first approached me about playing on the team, I knew nothing about basketball. More than anything, Coach Freeman helped me with self-esteem.

Once I started playing basketball, I began to develop

---

[4] Bid, 135.

some good friendships with kids who were involved with athletics and fell into a pretty typical high school life. I had a few girlfriends and enjoyed participating in activities associated with regular high school life. I went to dances, parties, and the prom, but I never felt like I fit in with any social group no matter how hard I tried.

I always felt like I was someone who was allowed to hang out with the group but not really part of the group and have wrestled with that feeling throughout most of my life. I think it has to do with feeling as though people view me as not quite normal. The thought of going to a high school reunion scares me even to this day. My biggest apprehension about joining Facebook was the fear of getting a friend request from someone from high school.

Oddly enough, about a year after my first draft of this chapter, I started receiving friend requests from high school friends. I have even mustered the courage to send a few friend requests. For some people this may seem like a small thing, but for me it was monumental. For the most part, it has been a good thing, and in ways, it has been healing.

Although I had some great times in high school, I don't look back on it as "the good old days." I spent a lot of time in dark corners. I drank way too much. I was the guy who was typically passed out or was throwing up in a friend's car. The best way to put it is that I was socially awkward, and I still am today in many regards. One of the most significant issues I have wrestled with throughout my life is trusting people. I live with this irrational fear that people will eventually hurt me in one way or another.

> One emotion that abuse victims have difficulty with is fear. A milder form of fear is distrust. Often, abused people will constantly question the motives of others. Since they have been mistreated in the past, they fear that everyone is

somehow out to take advantage of them again. More extreme examples are recurring nightmares, fear of abusing one's own children, fear that they are going to be abused by others, and vague, unexplained fears that "something bad is going to happen." Sometimes abuse victims will develop rituals in order to prevent the impending disaster they fear. These rituals lead to obsessive thought patterns and compulsive behavior.[5]

The excerpt above from Mic Hunter's book *Abused Boys* fits the story of my life perfectly. I just wish I had read it long before I was forty-four years old. For years after walking away from somebody or hanging up on the phone, my mind would immediately race through a litany of thoughts about what that person was thinking about me. If I had not seen someone for a long period of time, before visiting with that person, my stomach would be in knots at the apprehension of what that person thought about me. When I would walk away from people, quite often I had to tell myself not to turn around and that nothing was wrong. "Don't do it; just keep walking," I'd tell myself. This behavior has caused me to work way too hard at relationships, and more often than not I have sabotaged friendships because of my fears, which most often come across as trying too hard. I have spent most of my life analyzing and second-guessing other people's motives.

Oddly enough, unconsciously practicing this type of behavior has given me the ability to read people. I have been very successful in sales for a large part of my adult life, and I have been told by many people that I have an uncanny ability to read people very quickly. I am in tune

---

[5] Mic Hunter, *Abused Boys: The Neglected Victims of Sexual Abuse* (New York: Ballantine, 1990), 79.

with people's body language, the inflection in their voice, and their overall demeanor. It has been a great tool in my profession, but it has not helped me with friendships. On many occasions I have been told that I overthink things.

I developed OCD (obsessive-compulsive disorder)[6] long before it was in vogue. When the movie *As Good as It Gets* came out, Mary went to see it with a friend. She came home laughing and told me that she had just watched a movie about me. Released in 1997, the film is about a middle-aged, somewhat reclusive writer named Melvin Udall, played by Jack Nicholson, who suffers from OCD as well as a severe distrust of humanity. Melvin eats breakfast every morning in the same diner and is waited on by Carol Connelly, played by Helen Hunt. Carol waits on him every morning because she is the only waitress at the restaurant who can tolerate his strange and downright rude behavior.

Melvin begins to take an interest in Carol as the movie unfolds. The film does a great job of portraying some of the odd and frustrating behaviors exhibited by those who suffer from this disorder, such as extreme germaphobia, a fear of stepping on cracks in the sidewalk, door locking, hand washing, eating rituals, and counting, to name a few. The movie moves along the classic *Beauty and the Beast* storyline. Carol is the beautiful and caring woman who captures the heart of Melvin, the seemingly ugly and mean-hearted ogre. He is slowly forced out of his prison of dysfunction as the fear of losing Carol becomes more than he can bear, exposing the somewhat warm and caring soul trapped within.

My OCD began back in, junior high with nervous twitching and grunting. The twitching was typically jerk-

---

[6] "Obsessive-compulsive disorder (OCD)," *Mayo Clinic*, https://www.mayoclinic.org/diseases-conditions/obsessive-compulsive-disorder/symptoms-causes/syc-20354432.

ing my head back and forth or excessive blinking. These symptoms came and went with times of great stress. As you can imagine, they gave fuel to the other kids as something to make fun of, which made things worse. Counting began with the twitching and moved into other rituals.

Counting is an unfounded superstitious ritual developed by the fear that if something isn't done a certain way, bad things will happen. For example, if I didn't jerk my head back and forth three times after sitting down, I believed something bad would happen, Another manifestation is having to lock a door a certain number of times or having the seemingly uncontrollable compulsion to flip a light switch up and down a certain number of times before finally turning the lights off. This became really bad after I was married. I broke several door locks and door handles. Mary had no idea what was wrong with me. Can you imagine living with someone who feels the need to flick the lights on and off every time they go into or leave a room?

Counting is just one of the many manifestations that I exhibited. At the time I had never heard of obsessive-compulsive disorder. I still deal with the disorder, though with much less severity. Most people would never pick up on my habits unless they know me well or are watching closely. My family members will pick up on what am doing from time to time and let me know they have noticed by lovingly calling me Monk—meant as a lighthearted poke and often said with a roll the eyes, but always in fun.

I am assuming most people are familiar with the USA Networks series *Monk*, which depicts, in comedic fashion, a private detective, Adrian Monk, played by Tony Shalhoub, who suffers from OCD. It was a favorite around the Novack household for some time, based on a subject to which we all could relate. One of my favorite sayings is that "I'm not as bad as I once was, and I'm not as good as I hope to be one day," which I know I have mentioned previously and will most likely mention again.

Although I seemed to adjust to a somewhat typical teenage lifestyle in high school, sexually compulsive behavior continued to be an issue for much of my life. As sad as it is to say, it didn't make me much different than most of my friends. We lived in a culture immersed in sexuality. By the time I became a teenager in the early 1980s, the sexual revolution was in full swing. The movies we watched and the music we listened to were centered on sex, much as they are today. We were watching movies like *Fast Times at Ridgemont High* and *Porkies* and listening to "Hungry Like the Wolf" by Duran Duran, which is a song about a guy's relentless pursuit of "getting laid." Forgive the vulgar colloquialism, but it pretty well describes the state of mind of the average teenager with whom I was associated. We lived for the next party and "getting laid." Women were objectified from every angle in every media outlet, much like today. Pornography was everywhere in the form of magazines and videos. I went to parties with pornography playing on a VHS tape as the center of attention.

Student-teacher sexuality was also glorified. We jammed along to songs at our high school dances like "Hot for Teacher" by Van Halen and "Don't Stand so Close to Me" by the Police. We were aware of several inappropriate relationships between students and teachers, one of which was pretty well common knowledge, not well concealed, and it never stopped. Nobody ever went to jail or made the six o' clock news, but teachers from time to time were let go discreetly.

One day during my senior year, my friends and I were joking about the size of our penises during art class. My girlfriend was sitting at the table with us and was helping to add credence to my claim of enormous manhood. As the joking continued, my art teacher called me into the supply closet and closed the door. I thought he was going to reprimand me, but instead he wanted to see my penis. When I was hesitant, he explained that he wanted to see it because if it was as big as I said it was, we could make money doing pornographic movies.

He went on to tell me that he was regularly told that he had an average-sized penis but large balls that women loved. I clarified that my comments were just a joke and assured him that I had a very average-sized penis, hoping he would drop the subject. He did, and that was the end of the incident. The sad thing is, he didn't understand it was a joke. Was he so wrapped up in exploiting kids that he was hoping for an opportunity? Sadly enough, proven by his actions, he was. I regret never coming forward and reporting him. In the confusion of my life at that time, I lacked the maturity to understand or even consider the danger that he posed to other students.

Childhood sexual abuse is confusing. For so many of us it starts with friendship and a special feeling of inclusiveness. Many of us were made to feel special, taken to the side and spoken to in hushed tones of confidence and perhaps offered gifts. My art teacher pulled me aside and tried enticing me with the opportunity to make money and then tried creating a bond by telling me about something as personal as his genitals. The first time the older boy in my neighborhood approached me, we went to an out-of-the-way place, and he offered me money.

Most children may not be able to give a textbook definition of intimacy, but it is something that we all understand and desire. We are born with it indelibly imprinted in our DNA. We all want to feel special, and children are naturally curious and trusting. Children are easily seduced, which makes them especially vulnerable to sexual predation. Sexual abuse is not in any way a special or inclusive relationship. It is one person deceptively exercising dominance over a weaker and naïve person. Many of us were taken advantage of by people we looked up to or trusted. When writing about a boy who was molested by a priest, Dr. van der Kolk recounts the boy telling him, "Father Shanley was the closest thing to God in my neighborhood."[7]

Many of us feel deep shame and confusion because we feel we went along with our abusers, as if we were consenting participants. The truth is, no matter how shameful the situation, we have no reason to be ashamed. I will address the issue of shame head on in chapter twelve. For now, if you can relate to my story, I hope you can take comfort in the understanding that it is our story. The story that we share, however, is not just our story; it is the story of countless children around the world since the beginning of human history. Coming to this understanding does not make what happened to us OK, but if we will allow it, it can give us our next foothold in the struggle toward wholeness.

---

[7] van der Kolk, *The Body Keeps Score*, 176.

Chapter 8

Adverse Childhood Experience (ACE)

> Trauma is personal. It does not disappear if it is not validated. When it is ignores or invalidated the silent screams continue internally heard only by the one held captive.
>
> —Danielle Bernock,
> *Emerging With Wings: A True Story of Lies, And The Love that Heals*

There is a type of trauma that occurs as a slow, indelible burn. The relentless onslaught of small traumas, often referred to as "small t" traumas, are experienced by far too many children in this world—one would be too many. This is the type of pain associated with such things as the loss of a parent or living through a divorce, being incessantly put down or humiliated, or being physically or sexually abused. Children are overlooked, or the trauma occurs quietly in dark, shadowy recesses. This type of trauma is often ignored or minimized for many reasons, perhaps for the sake of keeping peace within the family or to avoid social embarrassment. Children's emotions are often regarded as secondary concerns and are all too often dismissed as issues that will straighten themselves out over time. Most people have heard someone say, "I wouldn't worry about it. Kids are resilient. He [or she] will bounce back in no time." As we will discuss, these notions are anything but true.

The majority of children have no idea that what they are going through is not "normal." One of the biggest reasons why this type of trauma goes unnoticed is because of the simple fact that most children have not developed a level of maturity that will allow them to understand their emotions or to recognize the simple fact that what is happening to them is wrong. Many adults have a hard time understanding what they are feeling, so how could we expect a child who does not understand his or her emotions to express what they are feeling inside? How many children go to the school nurse complaining of a stomach ache or some other physical discomfort when, in truth, they are overcome with anxiety?

One of the best chances that any of us have of overcoming the effects of trauma is to be surrounded by a loving and secure environment. How many children in this world have no idea what it is to be loved in a healthy way? For many children living in an atmosphere of security is as a foreign as living on Mars.

In 1985, Dr. Vincent Felitti observed something that would change how many people understood the correlation between childhood trauma and adult health issues. Felitti was chief of the world's largest medical screening program at Kaiser Permanente's Department of Preventive Medicine.

Felitti ran an obesity clinic using a technique called supplemental absolute fasting as a way for morbidly obese patients to lose weight through what they called Positive Choice Programs. He was shocked when he discovered that the majority of his patients had been sexually and/or physically abused as children. Within a very short period of time, several of the success stories from his program had regained their weight. Upon questioning one of his patients, he learned that after losing weight, she had gained the interest of a male coworker that made her very uncomfortable. Soon she felt it was safer to retreat back into her shell of security. Obesity had become a safe place of obscurity within a world where her life experiences had proven dangerous.

In 1990 Felitti took part in a meeting of the North American Association for the Study of Obesity, where he presented his findings from his team's first 286 interviews, only to receive sharp criticism from many of his colleagues. They felt that he was gullible for believing stories from his patients, that they were likely fabricated as an excuse for his patients' poor lifestyle choices. However, Felitti did gain the attention of Doctor Robert Anda, an epidemiologist from the Centers for Disease Control and Prevention (CDC). Felitti and Anda went on to develop what is known as the ACE study, which is now a well-known collaboration between the CDC and Kaiser Permanente.

They developed a questionnaire with ten questions that covered adverse childhood experiences, including physical and sexual abuse, physical and emotional neglect, and family dysfunction, such as having had parents who were divorced, mentally ill, addicted, or in prison.

A total of 17,421 patients took part in the study, and their answers were compared to extensive medical records kept by Kaiser Permanente. The results uncovered a remarkable correlation between ACEs (Adverse Childhood Experiences) and adult illness along with a list of self-destructive social and behavioral issues. The study also uncovered that ACEs are much more common in our world than understood.

My research led me to Donna Jackson Nakazawa's book *Childhood Disrupted: How Your Biography Becomes Your Biology, And How You Can Heal,* which I have quoted in previous chapters. This is one of those books that draws the reader in and does not let go. In 2012, Nakazawa, as she writes in her introduction, "came across a growing body of science based on a groundbreaking public health research study, the Adverse Childhood Experiences Study, or ACE Study."[1] She spent the next three years writing her book, as she recounts.

> I combed through seventy research papers that comprise the ACE Study and hundreds of other studies from our nation's best research institutions that support and complement these findings. And I followed thirteen individuals who suffered early adversity and later faced adult health struggles, who were able to forge their own life-changing paths to physical and emotional healing.[2]

Nakazawa's work does not just draw readers in because it is well written but because it is written with passion. She has not just put together a convincing case; as I turned the pages, it became clear that for her it was a deeply personal quest for the truth. She spent over a dozen years raising children in the grip of several autoimmune illnesses while at the same time working as a journalist. As she writes in her introduction, "My own doctor at Johns Hopkins medical institutions confessed to me that she suspected that, given the chronic stress I'd faced in my childhood, my body and brain had been marinating in toxic inflammatory chemicals my whole life—predisposing me to the diseases I now faced."[3]

I am thankful for Nakazawa's tenacity in the face of adversity and her willingness to share her story, a story that I hope that we will all tell one day. Not all of us who have experienced the adverse effect of traumatic stress in our lives will write books about our struggles, but I hope

---

[1] Donna Jackson Nakazawa, *Childhood Disrupted: How Your Biography Becomes Your Biology, and How You Can Heal* (New York: Atria, 2015), xiv.
[2] Ibid., xv.
[3] Ibid, 84.

we will all be able to share with others how we have overcome.

Below is the ACE survey. It is readily available on various websites. Most of the questionnaires that I have researched are fairly consistent in their wording, with only a few slight variations.

ADVERSE CHILDHOOD EXPERIENCES SURVEY

Prior to your eighteenth birthday:

1. Did a parent or another adult in the household often or very often swear at you, insult you, put you down, or humiliate you? Or act in a way that made you afraid that you might be physically hurt?

   Yes   No

   If yes, enter 1 _____

2. Did a parent or another adult in the household often or very often... push, grab, slap, or throw something at you? Or ever hit you so hard that you had marks or were injured?

   Yes   No

   If yes, enter 1 _____

3. Did an adult or person at least five years older than you ever touch or fondle you or have you touch their body in a sexual way? Or attempt to touch you or touch you inappropriately or sex-

ually abuse you?

Yes   No

If yes, enter 1 _____

4. Did you often or very often feel that no one in your family loved you or thought you were important or special? Or feel that your family members didn't look out for one another, feel close to one another, or support one another?

Yes   No

If yes, enter 1 _____

5. Did you often or very often feel that you didn't have enough to eat, had to wear dirty clothes, and had no one to protect you? Or that your parents were too drunk or high to take care of you or take you to the doctor if you needed it?

Yes   No

If yes, enter 1 _____

6. Was a biological parent ever lost to you through divorce, abandonment, or another reason?

Yes   No

If yes, enter 1 _____

7. Was your mother or stepmother often or very

often pushed, grabbed, slapped, or have something thrown at her? Or was she sometimes, often, or very often kicked, bitten, hit with a fist, or hit with something hard? Or ever repeatedly hit over the course of at least a few minutes or threatened with a gun or knife?

Yes   No

If yes, enter 1 _____

8. Did you live with anyone who was a problem drinker or alcoholic, or who used street drugs?

   Yes   No

   If yes, enter 1 _____

9. Was a household member depressed or mentally ill, or did a household member attempt suicide?

   Yes   No

   If yes, enter 1 _____

10. Did a household member go to prison?

    Yes   No

    If yes, enter 1 _____

    Add up your "Yes" answers: _____ (this is your ACE Score)

The following are statistics concerning ACE scores, as published in *Childhood Disrupted: How Your Biography Becomes Your Biology, And How You Can Heal.* Keep in mind your own score as we move along.

- People with an ACE score of 4 were twice as likely to be diagnosed with cancer as someone with an ACE Score of 0.[4]
- For each point an individual had, the chance of being hospitalized with an autoimmune disease in adulthood rose by 20 percent.[5] Take Kendall, with her ACE score of 6. According to Fairweather, Felitti, and Anda's research, Kendall's chance of having an autoimmune disease once she reached adulthood was 140 percent greater than that of a woman who had experienced no adverse childhood experiences at all. In fact, at age fifty-two, Kendall was diagnosed with three autoimmune diseases.[6]
- Someone with an ACE score of 4 was 460 percent more likely to be facing depression than someone with a score of 0.[7]
- An ACE score of 6 and higher shortened an individual's lifespan by almost twenty years.[8]
- Those with ACE scores of 7 or higher who didn't drink or smoke and who weren't overweight, diabetic, and didn't have a high cholesterol still had a 360 percent higher risk of heart disease than those with an ACE score of 0.[9]

---

[4] Ibid., 14.
[5] Ibid.
[6] Ibid., 99.
[7] Ibid., 14-15.
[8] Ibid., 15.
[9] Ibid.

- Eighteen percent of individuals with an ACE score of 1 suffered from clinical depression, and the likelihood rose sharply with each ACE point. Thirty percent of those with an ACE score of 3—and nearly 50 percent of those with an ACE score of 4 or more—suffered from chronic depression.[10]
- Nineteen percent of men with an ACE score of 1 suffered from clinical depression, and 24 percent of women with that score did. Likewise, while 24 percent of men with an ACE score of 2 developed adult clinical depression, 35 percent of women did.[11]
- Thirty percent of men with an ACE score of 3 developed clinical depression, compared to 42 percent of women who had three categories of adverse childhood experiences.[12]
- Thirty-five percent of men, versus nearly 60 percent of women, with an ACE score of 4 or more suffered from chronic depression.[13]
- Most disturbing are the statistics on suicide. While only 1 percent of those with an ACE score of 0 ever attempted suicide, almost 1 in 5 individuals with an ACE score of 4 or more had tried to end their lives. Indeed, a person with an ACE score of 4 or more was 1,220 percent more likely to attempt suicide than someone with an ACE score of 0.[14]
- Ten percent of men with an ACE score of 1 suffered from chronic depression, and 18 percent

---

[10] Ibid., 48.
[11] Ibid.
[12] Ibid.
[13] Ibid.
[14] Ibid.

of women did. Likewise, 33 percent of men with an ACE score of 4 or more later developed depression—already a high, disturbing figure—while nearly 60 percent of women with that score developing chronic depression in adulthood.[15]

A very relatable quote from Nakazawa's book comes from a young woman named Kat:

> "That completely surprised me," Kat says. She understood why she might have a hard time feeling happy as an adult, given what she'd been through growing up. But she never imagined that there could be a physiological connection "between what happened when I was five, and my immune system breaking down thirty years later."[16]

Here I sit at fifty-five years of age asking the same question. Could a series of events that began when I was a toddler be the reason why I have spent the past seven years with multiple trips to the emergency room and many nights in the ICU (Intensive Care Unit) with atrial fibrillation and heart arrhythmias? Could this be why I have made countless trips the Mayo Clinic trying to figure out why my nervous system is breaking down, being diagnosed with PTSD, a disruption in my autonomic nervous system diagnosed as cardiovagal failure, orthostatic intolerance, and irritable bowel syndrome? Is this why I was prescribed a BiPap Machine to use while I sleep so I don't stop breathing in the middle of the night?

---

[15] Ibid., 14.
[16] Ibid., 20–21.

The statistics speak for themselves. The answer is *yes*. It is very likely that my "biography" has become my "biology." What I wish I had known!

Chapter 9

The Two-way Street

> The parts of us that have been toxically shamed and split off reside in the subconscious.
>
> —John Bradshaw
> *Healing The Shame That Binds You*

Some in the mental health profession believe that stress and anxieties can somehow get trapped in the body or mind. I was very skeptical of this idea until I experienced a form of therapy called EMDR: Eye Movement Desensitization and Reprocessing. Most mental health professionals are very straightforward about the fact that they do not understand how these fragments of our past become trapped. Mental health is a fledgling science, and we still have much to learn, but for now it is enough for us to understand that our minds are complex and are capable of infinitely more than we understand.

Francine Shapiro developed EMDR by what she describes as "a chance discovery" in the spring of 1987 in her book, *Eye Movement Desensitization and Reprocessing (EMDR) Therapy*.

> While walking one day, I noticed that some disturbing thoughts I was having suddenly disappeared. I also noticed that when I brought these thoughts back to mind, they were not as upsetting or as valid as before. Previous experience had taught me that disturbing thoughts gener-

ally have a certain "loop" to them; that is, they tend to play themselves over and over until one consciously does something to stop or change them. What caught my attention that day was that my disturbing thoughts were disappearing and changing without any conscious effort.

Fascinated, I started paying very close attention to what was going on. I noticed that when disturbing thoughts came into my mind, my eyes spontaneously started moving very rapidly back and forth in an upward diagonal. Again, the thoughts disappeared, and when I brought them back to mind, their negative charge was greatly reduced. At that point I started making the eye movements deliberately while concentrating on a variety of disturbing thoughts and memories, and I found that these thoughts also disappeared and lost their charge. My interest grew as I began to see the potential benefits of this effect.[1]

Within a few days, Francine began trying her "chance discovery" on other people and began her first controlled study by the winter of 1987. In the beginning her primary focus was on reducing anxiety, so she called her new therapy Eye Movement Desensitization (EMD). She writes, " . . . for my first official study I wanted to find a homogeneous grouping of people who had difficulty with old memories. The people who first came to mind were rape victims, molestation victims, and Vietnam veterans who fit the diagnosis for PTSD."[2]

In 1990, after several years of case studies and support from other mental health professionals, Shapiro de-

---

[1] Francine Shapiro, *Eye Movement Desensitization and Reprocessing (EMDR) Therapy*, Third Edition, (New York, NY: Guilford Press, 2018), 7.
[2] Ibid., 8.

cided to change the name from EMD to EMDR.

> The continued refinement of these procedures and the subsequent evaluation of hundreds of case reports from trained clinicians led to the full realization that the optimal procedures caused the simultaneous desensitization and cognitive restructuring of memories, the elicitation of spontaneous insights, and an increase in self-efficacy, all of which appeared to be by-products of the adaptive processing of disturbing memories. This realization led to my renaming the therapy Eye Movement Desensitization and Reprocessing (EMDR).[3]

I first read of EMDR in Dr. Bessel van der Kolk's book, *The Body Keeps The Score*. The concepts seemed a little too simple and far-fetched. However, over the next several months, I discovered several other publications that touted EMDR therapy as being highly effective. I read through scores of testimonials by those who reported how it had significantly helped reduce the severity of their PTSD symptoms, and I became intrigued.

I soon found myself sitting on the couch (literally) of a therapist who practiced EMDR. As I move forward, I will be careful not to share too many details of my therapy. I am not trying to be guarded. We are all distinctive with our own personalities, and we all experience and perceive trauma differently. My concern is that I will build up false expectations for others. What I have experienced through therapy may not be what others experience. I am confident that the tools (different types of therapy) will work, but each practitioner will likely handle them a bit differently. As well, each person responds differently to therapy, and that is OK. We all have our own unique stories

---
[3] Ibid., 12.

that need to be told, and none of our roads will look exactly the same.

I often refer to my experience with EMDR as a trip down the rabbit hole.[4] I was not ready for what I experienced. My skepticism soon disappeared. I had no concept of how deeply the events of my past were affecting my present life until we began. By the end of the session, I was undone and holding a handful of tissues from the box on the table next to me. I didn't think much of that box when I sat down. I was in no way ready for the flood of all-but-forgotten memories that assailed my consciousness, things I hadn't thought of for years. Things I had spent a lifetime trying to forget. Yet there they were, waiting to emerge.

After leaving my therapist's office, I drove a short distance to get something to eat. As I sat in the parking lot eating my lunch, I tried to get a handle on what had just happened to me. When I sat down that day with my therapist, I was nervous and apprehensive about digging into my history of abuse, and within a few short minutes of starting, my focus had completely changed. The flood of memories that I experienced were not of my abuse but of all of the things that I have done to hurt other people and myself. My sin! That three-letter word that the world tries to ignore, and the church attempts to confess away. Jesus may have forgiven me, but my body was still keeping score.

EMDR had proven what St. Paul explained in his letter to the Romans almost two thousand years ago. "For I know that nothing good dwells within me, that is, in my flesh. I can will what is right, but I cannot do it. For I do not do the good I want, but the evil I do not want is what I do. Now if I do what I do not want, it is no longer I that do

---

[4] Lewis Carroll, *Alice's Adventures in Wonderland* (St. Martin's Street, London: Macmillan, 1912), 3.

it, but sin which dwells within me" (Romans 7:18–20).

"Sin" has become a dirty three-letter word in our society—in the world, for that matter—and understandably so. The word was meant to provoke an image of the sorrowful state of humanity wounded by the trauma of deception. Instead it has all too often been used as an insult or a sentiment of derision—a word used to dangle people over hell with a rotten stick.

Sin has become a word of intolerance when it should provoke compassion. My hope is that this word will begin to take on a new meaning as we continue. Just a slight shift in our understanding may change the way we perceive God. Let's begin by taking a look at another statement made by Dr. van der Kolk.

> Trauma, whether it is the result of something done to you or something you yourself have done, almost always makes it difficult to engage in intimate relationships. After you have experienced something so unspeakable, how do you learn to trust yourself or anyone else again? Or, conversely, how can you surrender to an intimate relationship after you have been brutally violated?[5]

"Trauma," the first word in the quote above, could have been replaced with the word "sin," and it would not have changed the meaning. All sin is trauma, but not all trauma is sin. For example, most traumatic accidents are not caused because of sin. The majority of accidents don't happen because of selfish intentions, as is the case with sin. Sins are committed because of misguided human desire. When we sin, we harm another or ourselves or both. Sexual sin almost always has two victims.

---

[5] Bessel van der Kolk, *The Body Keeps the Score: Brain, Mind, and Body in the Healing of Trauma* (New Your, NY: Penguin, 2015), 13.

When sin entered the world, it became the enemy of intimacy. Intimacy is the fuel that drives love. We were created for two reasons—to be loved and to love. The trauma of sin disrupts the flow of intimacy, thus diminishing our capacity not only to give love but also to receive it.

After Adam and Eve ate of the fruit of the Tree of the Knowledge of Good and Evil, they hid from God. The intimacy they shared with their Creator was gone. God wasn't simply angry; he was grieved. He was saddened, and He covered their shame and nakedness with compassion (Genesis 3). The message of the Cross of Christ is the redemption of humankind and the restoration of intimacy. It is compassion, not condemnation. Jesus did not come to dangle us over hell with a rotten sick. He came to restore intimacy and to heal His beloved Bride. (John 3:16)

There's a difference between being forgiven for our sins and being healed. Jesus is just in forgiving us of our sins through His blood (1 John 1:9). He is also able to heal us, but it doesn't always happen at the same time. Sin and trauma have natural consequences. We may be forgiven, but God is just. He doesn't free our conscience after hurting another person. People who have a clear conscience after hurting others are called sociopaths.

How would any of us feel if we went to a friend or a loved one after being hurt by that person and expressed how we felt, only to be dismissed? What if that person responded with, "I confessed what I did to God; therefore, you should just let it go and move on—I have"? I am using the absurd to illustrate the absurd. Of course confessing our sins to God doesn't remove all of the guilt and shame. Many of us try to move on and to live as if it does, and then we wonder why we can't shake our anxiety and guilt.

I have hurt several people who I am unable to approach to express the words that my heart aches to say: "I'm so sorry for hurting you." To do so would be irresponsible and selfish. They have moved on with their lives and have families. To intrude upon their lives could cause more damage than good. I have confessed what I have done to God, and I am confident that He has forgiven me. Now I need to trust Him at His word. Our Father assures us that one day, "He will wipe away every tear from their eyes, and death shall be no more, neither shall there be mourning nor crying nor pain any more, for the former things have passed away" (Revelation 21:4).

God may not heal us of all of our wounds on this side of Heaven. For now we can rest assured that in His perfect time, all things will be made right. Our part is to be as ready as humanly possible for when that day arrives, the day when we have the opportunity to look into the eyes of someone whom we have hurt and begin the healing. Equally as important, it is time to stop the poison. It is time to stop the hurt. Now that we know the truth, it is time to face the truth and indulge in the grace offered to us by God and no longer be instruments of sin or trauma (Romans 6:12–14). We may stumble from time to time, but we need to keep short accounts and learn to be quick to forgive and repent.

All the years of feeling that I had moved on from the sins and trauma of my past, only to discover I was carrying them around like so much unwanted baggage. This statement sounds terribly cliché, but my experience with EMDR proved that it is all too true.

Not all sin is incomprehensible trauma or what many in the mental health profession refer to as big "T" trauma. These are the major traumas that, if unrecognized or untreated, have the propensity to cause PTSD. Small t traumas are the far less traumatic offenses or bumps in the road of life that may seem somewhat harmless but can still contribute to the erosion of our well-being. The slow poison of small "t" trauma can inflict wounds that are just as toxic as big "T" trauma. Consider a parent who constantly criticizes and puts down a child. Regardless of whether we are dealing with the sin of big "T" or small "t" trauma, they both destroy the fabric of our being. The danger of small "t" trauma is that it often destroys one thread at a time, and before we are aware of what is happening the fabric of our being is seriously frayed.

When I was a child, my uncle molested me, which was unquestionably traumatic not only for me but also for my uncle. I am not trying to justify or sympathize with him, but there comes a time when we need to put away blame and engage in mature, rational discussion concerning our abuse. My uncle may have been the perpetrator, but I was not the only one traumatized. There is no question in my mind that my uncle was left wounded because of what he did.

Rabbit Trail

If you are aware of a child being abused, it must stop now! A child who is being abused must be separated from his or her abuser or abusers even if it requires contacting the legal authorities. In most cases the police should be involved. Child abuse is a crime and should be dealt with as such. I understand this may be a tough call, especially if it involves a family member, a friend, church member, or a pastor. A large percentage of children who are abused are abused by a trusted family member or friend. It is the child that should be protected, not the perpetrator.

With this being said, not every person who crosses the line sexually with a child is a pedophile. Sometimes things just happen, especially within the family dynamic. I have heard and read many stories of things that have happened involving a father, mother, or sibling that are one-time occurrences. Often, these occurrences cause a lifetime of grief for both the abused and the abuser. Even if it happens only once, it is still abuse and should not be swept under the rug. Therapy should begin as soon as possible, and strict boundaries must be established. A child's cry for help should never be ignored no matter how embarrassing or minor the situation may seem.

Back to the point:

My uncle's behavior, along with the actions of others, created unhealthy (sinful) sexual desires within me that inevitably led to sexual addictions. I have never molested a child, but I have traumatized other people because of my unhealthy sexual desires. I am the victim of sexual sin, but I am also a perpetrator.

Here are the big questions. What happened to my uncle to create the unhealthy sexual desire in his past? What happened to the older boy in my neighborhood? Were they molested as children? It's safe to say that most mental health clinicians would agree that there is a strong possibility that the answer to this last question is *yes*. Others would insist that there is no correlation between being the victim of childhood sexual abuse and going on to become a perpetrator. Many who hold this view believe that linking a history of childhood sexual abuse will create an unhealthy stigma around sex abuse victims, preventing those who need help from coming forward or being open about their abuse. It has certainly been a concern for me. I am very cautious around children. Although I have never had an inkling of a desire to molest a child, I live with the ever-present fear that one day something could happen because of the statistical evidence.

Over the years it has become evident that I had been

mentally and verbally abusive toward all of my children and Mary. Some may even argue that some of my methods of corporal punishment crossed the line. Much of my behavior was inherited, passed down from my parents. I, in turn, passed down what I learned to my children. I have heard it said that there is nothing worse than hearing your mother or father's words coming out of your mouth. What's worse is listening to your biting, controlling, and abusive words coming out of your children's mouths.

I cannot, however, blame all of my behavior on my parents. Much of my behavior was born out of fear of losing control. I can remember lying wide-awake in bed at night, paralyzed by the fear that I was losing control of one of my children. My fear wasn't born out of a need for control but out of a desire to protect them from the world that I experienced as a child. It was not until I learned about codependent behavior that I recognized my actions as manipulative and controlling.

Unresolved trauma rules our emotions and behavior and takes on a life of its own within our subconscious. Just as St. Paul explains in the scripture verse above, "it is no longer I that do it, but sin which dwells within me." If we are ever going to get past the effects of trauma and sin in our lives, we need to stop and turn to face our enemy head on.

King David, the only man in the Bible whom God described as having a heart after His own, wrote, "For I know my transgressions, and my sin is ever before me" (Psalm 51:3). David was quick to recognize and acknowledge his sin. When we read through the Psalms, it becomes clear that the man laid his heart out before God and the world.

If we are ever going to heal from the trauma and sin in our lives, we need to turn and face the truth and lay it all on the table. It is time to stop blaming our abusers and, just as importantly, forgive ourselves. Our abusers are not our enemy. Our enemy is the sin and trauma caused by the abuse. This may be incomprehensible for you right now, but it is the truth. Until you can forgive your abuser(s) and yourself, you will remain stuck in the mire of your past.

Many of us with a church background have been taught that all we need to do is go into a closet, close the door, ask for forgiveness, and all is forgotten. Here is what we need to understand: sin is not a private matter. The idea that we can slip away with God and confess our sins, is not only unbiblical, it's harmful. Yes, God forgives us when we confess our sins, but that is not the end of the thing. He loves us too much for that. The sins that we have committed have far-reaching consequences, just like the sins that have been committed against us.

Those of us who are afraid that our sin and trauma will be made known are living in a prison of our own making. The Bible teaches us that, "For nothing is covered that will not be revealed, or hidden that will not be known" (Mathew 6:26). You may be asking yourself, "Why would God expose my sins?" The answer is simple: because He loves us too much to leave us wounded. Consider the life of King David, a man scholars describe as one of the biggest scoundrels in the Bible. God laid David's sins bare in Sacred Scripture for generations to peruse at will. God loved David hard! David was God's beloved, and so are we. How many have found healing in David's words through the Psalms?

Whether we understand it or not, the sins that we commit wound us just as much as the sins committed against us. One of Israel's honorary names for God is Jehovah-Rapha, which means "Our God Who Heals." It is His nature to heal. When he sees one of his children in pain,

He reaches out and heals.

Many people are paralyzed at the thought of their sins being found out because of their misplaced need to hang on to anger. Whether we understand it or not, we are afraid we will be judged, just as we judge others. Consider the Lord's Prayer, "Forgive us our debts, as we also forgive our debtors" (Matthew 6:12). It's time for us to step out of the shadows and walk toward God with open hands. There is no greater desire in God's heart than to heal us from sin—to help us resolve the trauma of this life.

Let's take a look at what Sacred Scripture says about confessing our sins.

> Is any among you sick? Let him call for the elders of the church, and let them pray over him, anointing him with oil in the name of the Lord; And the prayer of faith will save the sick man, and the Lord will raise him up; and if he has committed sins, he will be forgiven. Therefore confess your sins to one another, and pray for one another, that you may be healed. (James 5:14–15)

The big takeaway that we should receive from the words above is that healing from sin and trauma is as important as being forgiven. Christ died for the forgiveness of the sins of the world. He took the penalty of our sins upon Himself. By His stripes we are healed (Isaiah 53:5). He made it possible for the healing to begin through forgiveness, but we are active participants in the healing process. When we learn to forgive from our hearts, we become healers—not only of others but also ourselves.

The Bible says that when we receive Christ, we become joint heirs with Him, "provided we suffer with him in order that we may also be glorified with him" (Romans

8:17).

There is nothing more healing than confessing our sins to another and hearing that we are loved and forgiven. If you are Catholic or Orthodox, start by going to confession. If not, find your pastor or a counselor. God is waiting in Heaven for His prodigals to come, so He can run and heal us of our unresolved trauma (Luke 15:20).

Confessing our sin and discussing our trauma with a pastor is a good place to start, but don't stop there. Find a good counselor who specializes in PTSD and grief counseling. I understand that what I have written above may feel like a ten-ton steel ball. Not only do we lack the strength to carry the thing, we also have no idea of where to grab hold of it. It doesn't even appear to have handles.

That's OK. When I started this journey toward recovery, I was angry and confused. I had no idea that the ten ton-steel ball existed. So, just start at the beginning. You do not need to travel this road alone.

Most important is that we learn to live the life of the beloved, as Aundi Kolber states, "During our hardest, scariest times—whether our bodies feel stressed and jumpy or sluggish and slow—God is there to reassure us that we are not defined by our best days or our worst days. We are his beloved."[6]

---

[6] Aundi Kolber, *Try Softer: A Fresh Approach to Move us out of Anxiety, Stress, and Survival Mode—and into a Life of Connection and Joy* (Carol Stream, Illinois: Tyndale House, 2020), 72.

Chapter 10

Pornography Addiction and Healing

> The areas in which we felt most insecure, unsafe, unloved, uncomfortable, embarrassed, angry, and generally unresolved as a child are the areas that we will be most prone to self-deception as an adult.
>
> — Cortney S. Warren,
> *Lies We Tell Ourselves:
> The Psychology of Self-Deception*

The subject of sexual addiction is almost unavoidable when addressing the issue of childhood sexual abuse. Almost all children who have been sexually abused suffer from some type of sexual confusion, which often leads to addiction. For many it begins with incessant masturbation, uncontrolled sexual promiscuity, or both.

Dr. van der Kolk, shares his observations at a treatment center he attended for abused children.

> Having a biological system that keeps pumping out stress hormones to deal with real or imagined threats leads to physical problems: sleep disturbances, headaches, unexplained pain, oversensitivity to touch or sound. Being so agitated or shut down keeps them from being able to focus their attention and concentration. To relieve their tension, they engage in chronic

masturbation, rocking, or self-harming activities (biting, cutting, burning, and hitting themselves, pulling their hair out, picking at their skin until it bled). It also leads to difficulties with language processing and fine-motor coordination. Spending all their energy on staying in control, they usually have trouble paying attention to things, like schoolwork, that are not directly relevant to survival, and their hyperarousal makes them easily distracted.[1]

As I sit and consider the dialectical narrative of my life, the first question that comes to mind is, "What if I had known?", followed by, "How much of a difference would it have made?" As I read paragraphs like the one above, I can't help but wonder how could a child whose shell of security being abruptly shattered by sexual abuse possibly understand feelings meant to be reserved for adulthood.

When men or women are asked why they feel they are addicted to pornography, the answers may vary, but when it comes right down to it, many have no idea why. How can anyone who has spent their entire life ignoring and running away from their emotions tell you how they feel? Most addicts relate to feeling good or being angry or uncomfortable. Ask an addict how they feel when they are sad or experiencing grief. Most will express themselves in terms of anger. All they understand is that they are uncomfortable and want to feel better at any cost.

As Aundi Kolber shares in her book, *Try Softer*,

> Sometimes in my clinical practice, clients tell me heart-wrenching accounts of pain and abuse, but when I ask them to describe their

---

[1] Bessel van der Kolk, *The Body Keeps the Score: Brain, Mind, and Body in the Healing of Trauma* (New Your, NY: Penguin, 2015), 160.

emotions, they cannot do it—they simply cannot articulate how they feel. At other times, people have barely begun to share their stories when they dissolve in floods of tears and explode in outbursts of anger.[2]

I have dealt with sexual addiction for most of my life. My addiction has been with pornography. At times when life seemed to be good, my addictive behavior would wane and even become seemingly non-existent. But as soon as things got a little tough, my addiction would jump back onto the scene as if it were poised and waiting in the wings for the perfect opportunity to steal the spotlight. I spent the first four decades of my life not understanding or being willing to admit I had a sexual addiction. I would listen to other men talk about their pornography addiction and think, *That's not me. I can put it away at any time I like.*

At age forty-three, when my life seemed to be falling apart, and for the first time in almost four decades I began to confront my childhood abuse, pornography became the addiction I never imagined possible. I had no idea of how to deal with my emotions.

Let's take a look at what Dr. Kevin B Skinner says about this issue in his book, *Treating Pornography Addiction: The Essential Tools for Recovery:*

> Our emotions are the internal indicators that tell us how we are doing. Sadly, when most people are experiencing these emotions they do not know how to resolve them so they turn to some form of misbehavior (e.g., pornography, abuse, substance abuse, reckless behavior, etc.).

---

[2] Aundi Kolber, *Try Softer: A Fresh Approach to Move us out of Anxiety, Stress, and Survival Mode—and into a Life of Connection and Joy* (Carol Stream, Illinois: Tyndale House, 2020), 118.

In our society we seldom teach people how to deal with feelings of sadness, loneliness, boredom, frustration, anger, or other negative emotions. As a result, most people turn to quick fixes because it is not fun to stay in a state of being emotionally frustrated. When emotions are not dealt with in appropriate ways relapse is the likely outcome. Some of the common emotions that lead to relapse include:

- Curiosity
- Need for excitement
- Frustration/stress
- Irritation
- Anger
- Boredom
- Pain
- Loneliness
- Worry
- Fear

Far too often people live in a state of emotional numbness. This comes from a lack of knowing how to resolve problems. When we do not know how to solve something our mind wants to take us to a place of safety, but when we are in this mindset we simply survive rather than thrive. Survival is the primary mechanism in all of us, which is why we flee into safety when we do not know how to solve problems. Safety is the place we go when the answers to our problems are not easily solved. For people dealing with pornography addiction, they are in safety when they allow feelings of hopelessness and helplessness guide their behaviors. At this point they give up on trying to overcome their addiction and say there is nothing they can do to win the battle.[3]

Before I began facing my past, the Christian subculture of which I was a part insisted that our emotions are unreliable—believing that the flesh (the heart) is not to be trusted and should be considered the enemy of the spirit. I have sat through countless hours of Christian counseling discussing my behavior or how God or my wife felt, but oddly enough, we seldom, if ever, discussed how I felt.

Without question, pornography is sinful, but the cure for this addiction is not shame any more than shame is the solution for lust. The antidote to lust is contentment, and contentment is born out of trust and faith. I will discuss trust and faith in much more detail in chapter thirteen. Shame does nothing more than fan the flames of confusion. I have suffered through countless sermons, listening to well-intended pastors beating the life out of the ones they are trying to help.

The majority of men who are addicted to pornography are not addicted because they do not love their wives, cherish other women, or find other women more attractive than their wives or girlfriends. Sexual addiction is primarily emotional, and as long as we continue to treat our emotions as the enemy, we will continue to fan the flames of confusion concerning this issue. The good news is that I have since discovered many Christian counselors and pastors who understand how important our feelings and emotions are to God. Let me assure you, dear reader, God loves you and does not consider the way you feel to be the enemy of His spirit.

Most men or women who have been sexually abused watch pornography because they have no idea of how to

---

[3] Kevin B. Skinner, *Treating Pornography Addiction: The Essential Tools for Recovery* (Provo, Utah: Growth Climate, 2005), Kindle locations 1469–1480.

deal with the discomfort of their emotions and are seeking a way of feeling better. I realize this statement may sound paradoxical, but please hang in there with me as I attempt to explain. The incessant masturbation and the uncontrolled promiscuity that I discussed at the beginning of this chapter activates the pleasure center in the brains of prepubescent children, creating a conditioned response. Thoughts of the very act that caused trauma (sexual abuse) can provoke sexual arousal and even pleasure. This behavior becomes confusing as these children reach adolescence and adulthood and nurtures an identity of shame and self-loathing.

This addiction goes way beyond an emotional need. It creates a chemical dependency that can be more debilitating than drugs or alcohol. Dr. Kevin B. Skinner explains.

> Dr. Patrick Carnes, a renowned sexual addiction counselor, reported in his research with over 1,000 individuals that sex addictions are more challenging to overcome than drugs or alcohol. Dr. Carnes writes, "We have learned that addictive obsession can exist in whatever generates significant mood alteration, whether it be the self-nurturing of food, the excitement of gambling, or the arousal of seduction. One of the more destructive parts of sex addiction is that you literally carry your own source of supply." What this means is that the brain naturally produces chemicals. Unlike any drug or alcohol substance, our own internal chemistry produces the addictive chemicals while viewing pornography, and these chemicals are very addictive when they are abused. We can get high on our own internal brain chemicals.[4]

---

[4] Ibid., Kindle locations 570-571.

There were days when I couldn't wait to go into my office, shut the door, and feel the chemicals coursing through my body. I would click from image to image, trying to find that perfect scenario that would excite me to the point of ecstasy and free me from my pain. The problem with any drug is that we can never reach the high for which we are hoping. It is a search for something that does not exist.

What we seek to free us is, in reality, is nothing but a never-ending torment (unless we can get the help we need). I would sit and watch for hours, never allowing myself physical release because I knew the chemicals in my body would dissipate as soon as it happened. Well into my addiction, I would watch image after image and never have an erection. It is an addiction like any other. At first it entices through excitement. Then it binds with chemical dependency, finally leaving its victim in a relentless pursuit of something he or she will never attain.

In the quote above, Dr. Carnes says, "One of the more destructive parts of sex addiction is that you literally carry your own source of supply." Someone who is addicted to pornography doesn't need to be hidden way in a dark corner watching a computer screen to escape reality. He or she can play any video they like in the dark reassess of their minds, or right up front, for that matter. They can fantasize about sex anywhere and about anyone they want.

I have spent hours releasing endorphins and other chemicals into my body while driving my car or, sadly enough, lying in bed next to my wife. It becomes a seemingly never-ending condition-response sequence. The moment I felt the slightest bit of discomfort, my mind would think about sex, and my body would receive the drugs it was craving. This cycle becomes so automatic in the life of an addict that recovery becomes a seemingly ceaseless battle. Trust me, as impossible as it may seem at times, complete recovery is entirely possible.

When the memories and pain of the past return and collide with the present, our minds seek what we knew as children as a way of comfort, even well into adulthood. Picture a boy of eight or nine years old. It's bedtime, and the lights go out. He is all alone, "uncomfortable," and most likely has no understanding of why. The boy doesn't suck his thumb for comfort or rub the corner of his blanket like many children do. Instead, he rubs himself, masturbating, because it is soothing. He doesn't always know why or consider how he learned such a thing. Somehow his mind has become wired that way. In the darkness of the night, the boy will continue to short-circuit the wiring of his mind, having no idea of the chaos he is creating for his future.

Envision this small hurting boy, years later, now living in an adult body, but he has never learned to deal with his feelings. As with all addictions, the demand for the anesthetizing drug becomes ever greater, whether ingested or supplied by the body.

How do we stop the addiction? How do we break this deeply imbedded cycle? First, we need to see sexual addictions for what they are—a form of dissociation. Addictions take us out of our present moment, just as the mind uses dissociation. As the mind feels the need to dissociate to protect the person, the addict feels the need for an endorphin release. In the addict's mind, when he or she becomes uncomfortable with feelings the addict does not understand or is not willing to deal with, he or she needs a way to find relief. To the addict, these are not just merely desires; they are needs that will be sought at any cost, like a drowning man seeks for air.

We also need to understand that sexual addictions are traumatic and sinful. I understand that there is a movement to normalize perverse behavior in an attempt to render it somehow less shameful. No matter how hard some may try, pornography, infidelity, and every other sexual sin will always be shameful and destroy our capacity for intimacy and love. The pornography industry is devastating to everyone it touches or influences. It destroys the lives of the men and women involved in its production and is just as destructive in the lives and families of those who are addicted.

So, how do we become free of sexual addiction? The answer is simple—the truth! However, getting to the truth is the difficult part. We must learn to be completely honest with ourselves about our past and the way we feel. This is where the hard work begins—learning to deal with our emotions. Many of us have developed an intricate narrative, also referred to as a "cover story," concerning our past. These are the lies that we have created to hide our shame from the world and ourselves. Remember that "other self" from chapter three whom we banished to the "dark places of our heart," when we discussed dissociation? We begin the steps toward freedom when we turn the key in the lock.

Here is a pearl of wisdom that Dr. van der Kolk learned from one of his college professors.

> Semrad taught us that most human suffering is related to love and loss and that the job of therapists is to help people acknowledge, experience, and bear' the reality of life—with all its pleasures and heartbreak. **'The greatest sources of our suffering are the lies we tell ourselves,"** he'd say, urging us to be honest with ourselves about every facet of our experience. He often said that people can never get better without knowing what they know and

feeling what they feel.[5]

I get into the subject of our emotions in much greater detail in chapter twelve. For now I will say that you need to learn to recognize your triggers and when a trigger has been pulled without you realizing it. Some of these triggers can be subtle. Stop and ask yourself, "What is happening here? Why are these fantasies running in my head? Why am I being tempted to take things a little too far while surfing the Internet? Why do I feel compelled to participate in something that, a day ago or even an hour ago, I so desperately wanted to be free from?"

I don't need to tell a single addict reading this that such behavior needs to stop. Sexual addiction is a slow, painful torment. The only way to stop the torment is to dig in and begin the hard, grueling, and unavoidably painful work of recovery. This is a temptation that I still wrestle with. At times I find my mind drifting off into places it shouldn't, or I see an image on social media or the Internet that triggers a desire to see more. When this happens, stop, dig deep, and ask yourself what is happening. Why are you so uncomfortable?

Aundi Kolber talks about staying within our "window of tolerance" concerning our emotions.[6] In other words, not ignoring your emotions and "white knuckling" your way through life.[7] This is the stuff of dissociation.

> The space between hyper- and hypoarousal, what might be thought of as the "just right" amount or intensity, is the range in which we can experience emotions, sensations, and experiences without feeling physiologically overwhelmed. First named by Dr. Daniel Siegel but

---

[5] van der Kolk, *The Body Keeps Score*, 26–27.
[6] Kolber, *Try Softer*, 72.
[7] Ibid., 5.

additionally strengthened through the work or Dr. Stephen Porges, this range is our window of tolerance (WOT). Each of us has a WOT, whether we find we are constantly pushing against the edges of it or not. When we are in our window, the brain stays integrated with the prefrontal cortex, which allows up to pay compassionate attention to our selves and to try softer. This is where we want to be.[8]

Paying attention to your emotions is paramount to our recovery. When you learn to be honest with yourself and mindful of how you are feeling, life just might begin to work. I understand this may be an entirely new experience.

Let me assure you, dear reader, that recovery is a long, exhausting battle, but it is so worth the fight. Shame is self-perpetuating; it deadens the senses and destroys hope. When we lose hope, we have lost it all. As difficult as it may be to remember in the despair and hopelessness of our addictions, God never loses hope in us. He stands on the balcony of heaven and waits in expectation for His children, so He can run to us the moment we turn (St. Luke 15:20). He sent His beloved Son into this world to rescue us from the trauma and sin of this life and bring us home. As impossible as it may be to understand at times, we are His beloved.

The paragraph above was just as much for me as it is for you. I don't know if any of us who live in the wake of abuse and battle with sexual addiction have any idea of the weight of grief upon our souls.

"She had not known the weight, until she felt the freedom!" (Nathaniel Hawthorne, *The Scarlet Letter*) Aundi Kolber uses the above quote to open chapter four of her

---

[8] Ibid., 72.

book, *Try Softer*. This simple quote jumped off the page the first time I read it and continues to grow in my heart, just like the words of Kolber's book. I have read tens of thousands of pages of information on the subjects of abuse, trauma, PTSD, and healing over the past twelve years, and few books, if any, have watered my soul like *Try Softer*.

I have spent decades trying to prove to God that I am worthy of His love, only to feel like a failure again and again through my self-destructive behavior. How could I dare to believe that God could ever consider me His beloved? I have looked toward God with the shadow of my conscience obscuring my understanding of Him for most of my life (James 1:17).

God never takes His gaze off us. He never stops longing for his children to emerge from the shadows and embrace Him for who He truly is as they begin to understand who they are in Him.

We are His beloveds, and He is ours (Song of Solomon 2:16).

Chapter 11

Sexual Dysfunction

> Shame is a soul eating emotion.
>
> —Carl Gustav Jung

Sexual dysfunction is a condition that has become common in our overstressed world for both men and women. Difficulties in the bedroom can be stressful in and of itself and the cause for deep-seated shame. These difficulties can occur for many reasons. However, for this discussion, I will be focusing on sexual dysfunction as it is related to PTSD.

The primary reasons for sexual dysfunction have long been thought to be anxiety, depression, or any number of psychological conditions. This opinion is slowly starting to change as science uncovers evidence that the cause may not be purely psychological but also neurological. The same shift in understanding occurred with our understanding of PTSD in the middle and latter part of the twentieth century.

Sexual dysfunction is likely as common with women who suffer with PTSD as it is with men. Women typically experience symptoms such as vaginal dryness, pain during intercourse, and a disinterest in sex, among others. Unfortunately, there is little data available pertaining to women suffering with this issue. Most of the data available concerning sexual dysfunction as it pertains to dysautonomia or PTSD focuses on men, specifically on ED (erectile dysfunction) and PE (premature ejaculation).

I will be focusing primarily on ED and PE for the remainder of this chapter, but for my female readers, I have no doubt that you suffer right along with the men, if not more. If we had accurate statistics for females who are molested as children and also raped or sexually harassed as adults the numbers would be mind staggering. An online article published by the US Department of Veterans Affairs states that nearly 24 percent of female Veterans seeking VA healthcare report a history of military sexual trauma. I was stunned the first time I read this statistic. The same article reports,

> In one study, of male combat Veterans diagnosed with PTSD, for example, 85 percent reported erectile dysfunction, compared with a 22 percent rate among male combat Veterans without any mental health diagnosis. Another study of 90 male combat Veterans with PTSD found more than 80 percent were experiencing sexual dysfunction.[1]

Unfortunately, most published information on the subject of ED does not differentiate between ED and PE. PE is included with the ED statistics. PE is thought to be the more prevalent form of ED,[2] which can be misleading because many understand ED as the inability to achieve an erection. Consider the slogan for Viagra, the little blue pill "that helps guys with erectile dysfunction get *and keep an erection*." There are also reports implicating the occurrence of spontaneous ejaculation with men suffering

---

[1] "Sexual dysfunction a common problem in Veterans with PTSD," *US Department of Veterans Affairs*, March 24, 2015,
https://www.research.va.gov/currents/spring2015/spring2015-3.cfm.
[2] C. Carson & K. Gunn, "Premature ejaculation: definition and prevalence," *International Journal of Impotence Research*, Sept. 5, 2006,
https://www.nature.com/articles/3901507.

with PTSD.[3] Spontaneous ejaculation is an emission that occurs with no apparent physical or mental stimulation.

A May 16, 2018, Mayo Clinic article titled "Premature Ejaculation" states that "as many as 1 out of 3 men say that they experience this problem at some time."[4]

The article goes on to list the following physiological factors that may play a role in premature ejaculation.

- Early sexual experiences
- Sexual abuse
- Depression
- Worrying about premature ejaculation
- Guilty feelings that increase your tendency to rush through sexual encounters

Now we will explore the physiological and neurological aspects of an erection and how ED and PE come into play with those suffering with PTSD. To begin, let's take a look at an excerpt from an article titled "Erectile Dysfunction as a Sign of Dysautonomia" by Dr. Derrick Lonsdale:

> As has been described in the pages of this website many times, the autonomic nervous system (ANS) is almost completely automatic and is governed by controls in the limbic system of the brain and the brainstem. It consists of two major components, the sympathetic and parasympathetic systems. These two branches of the ANS always work in concert, emphasizing the "do's" and "don'ts" of body functions. In or-

---

[3] Taner Öznur, Süleyman Akarsu, Bülent Karaahmetoğlu, & Ali Doruk, "A rare symptom in posttraumatic stress disorder: Spontaneous ejaculation," *American Journal of Case Reports*, Feb. 14, 2014,,
https://www.amjcaserep.com/download/index/idArt/889658.
[4] "Premature Ejaculation," *Mayo Clinic*, last accessed Dec. 1, 2020,
https://www.mayoclinic.org/diseases-conditions/premature-ejaculation/symptoms-causes/syc-20354900.

der to become erect, the arterial blood is pumped into erectile tissue in the penis and the venous return is occluded. This action is under the control of the sympathetic branch of the ANS, while ejaculation is under the control of the parasympathetic branch. Obviously, this is complex because the two branches have to be able to coordinate their activity. That is why ED is a symptom of dysautonomia, a condition that may present with a variety of seemingly unrelated symptoms. These include: fatigue, difficulty concentrating, orthostatic intolerance, heart palpitations, constipation or diarrhea, poor appetite or early satiety, urinary retention or incontinence and, as we have pointed out, ED. Failure to connect the diverse symptoms with a single underlying mechanism may lead to incorrect diagnoses, inappropriate interventions and frustration on the part of both doctors and patients.[5]

You may have noticed that Dr. Lonsdale uses some of the same terminology that I covered in chapter four when I discussed the limbic system and the role of the autonomic nervous system. You'll recall that one of the regions within the limbic system is the hypothalamus, which is responsible for signaling the body to release hormones. The hypothalamus not only releases stress hormones, it is also responsible for controlling sexual arousal, physical performance of the genitals,[6] and ejaculation. Researchers are beginning to think the hypothala-

---

[5] Derrick Lonsdale, "Erectile Dysfunction as Sign of Dysautonomia," *Hormones Matter*, March 11, 2019, https://www.hormonesmatter.com/erectile-dysfunction-dysautonomia/.
[6] Irwin Goldstein, "The Central Mechanisms of Sexual Function," *Boston University School of Medicine—Sexual Medicine*, August 20, 2020,
https://www.bumc.bu.edu/sexualmedicine/publications/the-central-mechanisms-of-sexual-function/.

mus is involved with the issue of premature ejaculation.[7] It is likely that the same communication glitch that is responsible for the dysautonomia experienced by many of us suffering from PTSD may also be responsible for sexual dysfunction.

There is undeniable evidence that a statistically large number of men who watch pornography suffer from ED or PE. There is a growing dispute in the mental health and medical communities as to the cause. One school of thought is that the issue may be the same as with any other addiction—the longer the addict watches, the more he will need to be satisfied, just like drug users requiring increased amounts of whatever substance they are addicted to achieve release. Those on the other side of this argument claim there is no correlation between watching pornography and ED. They do, however, reluctantly admit that a large number of users suffer with ED, but they claim that pornography is not the cause.[8] They assert various reasons such as underlying mental health issues or religious or social beliefs that cause shame.

As I discussed in chapter ten, there is an ever-present effort in our world to minimize the effects of shame by attempting to normalize immoral behavior. An alarming number of mental health professionals promote this philosophy. It seems they are blinded to the truth regardless of the overwhelming evidence that shame is toxic. They seem to feel that shame is an obstacle to be overcome or neutralized, rather than a gift given to us by our Creator as a healthy boundary marker allowing us to live a happy, healthy, and productive life within His natural order.

---

[7] Ming Gao et al., "Altered Functional Connectivity of Hypothalamus in Lifelong Premature Ejaculation Patients," *JMRI*, February 18, 2020, https://onlinelibrary.wiley.com/doi/abs/10.1002/jmri.27099.
[8] Joshua B. Grubbs & Mateusz Gola, "Is Pornography Use Related to Erectile Functioning? Results From Cross-Sectional and Latent Growth Curve Analyses," *Elsevier*, 2018, https://www.seksuologen-vlaanderen.be/wp-content/uploads/2019/06/Grubbs-Gola-2019-J-SEX-MED-no-causal-link-pornography-and-ED-2.pdf.

New York Times bestselling author John Bradshaw discusses the idea of toxic shame in his book *Healing the Shame That Binds You*. He says, "If we are continually overexposed, shame becomes toxic."[9] He goes on to address shame and sexuality by stating,

> As the sex drive fully emerges, the feeling of shame becomes more activated than at any other time in the life cycle. The initial experience of sexuality is one of awe and strangeness. Today we have lost what the ancients called the phallic and vaginal mysteries. Thomas Moore writes poignantly about the mystery of sexuality in his book The Soul of Sex. In our shameless culture, sex has been depersonalized. It has become a fact, not a sacred value. Parents need to model and teach an awe and reverence for their own and their children's sexuality.
>
> Nature has made the sexual experience the most exciting and pleasurable of all our experiences. Nature wants us to mate and procreate. Sex and shame go hand in hand because we need our sense of shame as a boundary for our sexual desires.[10]

Shame is the biggest reason for mental illness today, just as it has been since Adam and Eve took their first breath. Childhood sexual abuse creates shame like few other experiences. It is a violation that robs us of what was meant to be one of our greatest gifts—the innocence and "awe" of sexuality. All too often, this gift becomes a lifetime of confusion and suffering—a life forever altered before we possess the maturity to understand what has

---

[9] John Bradshaw, *Healing The Shame That Binds You* (Deerfield Beach, Florida: Health Communications, 1988, revised 2005), 11.
[10] Ibid., 15–16.

happened to us.

Pornography and other forms of sexual addiction continue to steal from us, pushing the boundaries of our sexuality and causing toxic shame, which is trauma. Every person knows the difference between right and wrong, good and evil (Genesis 2). Whether we acknowledge our understanding of right and wrong or not, it is deeply embedded within the fabric of humanity. It is inescapable, and denying the truth will not deliver us from shame.

So, how do we heal from sexual dysfunction? This is a question I have long asked myself. I think the best way to answer this question is with another question: who do we believe we are as people?

If we listen to the world, we will hear the message that we are sexual beings. Sex is an amazing gift from our Creator, but it does not define us. The truth is that we are spiritual beings created to be loved and to love. We are created for intimacy, but sex is not intimacy. Sex outside the boundaries of God's natural order destroys intimacy.

If you have been sexually abused or traumatized and suffer with sexual dysfunction, shame should have no place in your life. Start healing by taking yourself off the hook. We may heal physically from sexual dysfunction, but true healing begins when we come to a place where we learn the joy of true intimacy. I have wrestled with feelings of inadequacy and shame for years. Beginning when I was a small child, the world taught me that sex is the end game. It also taught me some confusing things about what it means to be a man and to have value.

Real intimacy happens without sex. When we are truly intimate with someone, we experience the greatest joy of this life. How many of us never experience true joy because we believe the deception of this world? So many of us have been blinded to the fact that we have been robbed of the authentic life that we are meant to live.

Many of us are driven deeper into shame by trying to fix something that is not broken. We may appear to be broken physically when the real problem is in our minds and in our spirits. We need to stop focusing on the physical and begin the hard work of healing emotionally. I will continue to discuss emotional healing in the next few chapters. You may be surprised if you start experiencing physical changes as you begin to heal emotionally and experiencing the life that God intended for each one of us. The important thing is that we stop our shameful behavior, remember that sexual dysfunction is nothing to be ashamed of, and begin to have compassion for ourselves.

Chapter 12

Untying the Knots of Our Emotions

> Compassion is the antidote to shame. As it is with most poisons, the toxicity of shame needs to be neutralized by another substance if we are truly going to save the patient.
>
> — Beverly Angel

During my recovery I learned about rooms in my heart that I never knew existed. Soon after I began the process of dealing with my past, weeping became a daily occurrence. It was as if I were filled with tears and that if I tilted my head just slightly, they would come running out. It was like so many years of anger and shame were pouring out of me in waves of grief.

I would be out in public at a restaurant or in a store, and people would give me odd looks. Someone even asked me if something was wrong with me because I was continuously drying my eyes. Even when I was not thinking about anything to be upset about, the tears would flow. My weeping was accompanied by episodes of uncontrollable sobbing, at times seemingly unprovoked. I started to wonder if I was losing my mind. Sometimes I even woke up from a sound sleep and found myself sobbing.

I was forty-three years old and had emotions pouring out of me, but I had no idea how to deal with them. I have always been an emotional person. I cry during television commercials and have suffered from feelings of anxiety, depression, and anger for most of my life, but I had no idea how to process what was happening.

Recovery became an exploration of my emotions. I was sailing into uncharted waters. I had no idea what I would discover, but I jumped in with both feet.

During my recovery, I joined the Catholic Church. God knew exactly where I needed to be and when. The church I attended while going through RCIA (Rite of Christian Initiation for Adults) was pastored by a charismatic Franciscan priest. I met with him for counseling on many occasions during my recovery. Something happened during one of those sessions that I will never forget. As was his habit, during one of our meetings he laid one hand on my head and the other on my shoulder and prayed. As he began to pray, I began to weep. When he realized what was happening, he leaned over and asked me what I was feeling. This may seem like a small thing to some, but to me it was life-changing. Sure, I have had other people ask me how I was doing, typically in passing, but when he asked me, I had an overwhelming sense that he actually cared how I was feeling.

I will never forget my reaction. I just looked at him for a few moments and then repeated the question, "How do I feel?" As I pondered the question, I became overwhelmed, struggling to catch my breath. "Holy shit!" I said when I was finally able to respond. "How do I feel? What does how I feel have to do with any of this?" He did not get offended or change his tone. Instead, without missing a beat, he asked me again, "Yeah, what are you feeling?" The question was so different from anything I had ever experienced from a pastor or even from another human being.

At that point in our meeting, as had been my experience with pastoral counseling, I was expecting to be sitting in front of an open Bible and listening to the priest read Scripture verses that would remind me that God had everything under control and that my being upset was counterproductive and displayed a lack of faith.

The tears continued to flow as I processed the question. I had no idea how to answer, but somehow in that moment God became a person to me. I had known that God loved me, and I had often felt His love in a tangible way, but this was something different. This man of God never opened his Bible. He had just shown genuine concern for how I was feeling, and it was amazing. It spoke of God's love for me more than a thousand sermons ever could. I was experiencing compassion, a word I had heard countless times throughout my life but had no real understanding or experience of.

The Cords of Our Emotions

I soon began to envision our emotions as cords that travel through the fabric of our being. These emotions become so entangled that without careful scrutiny we have little hope of understanding where one starts and another ends. Some of these emotions, such as love and hate, travel in pairs. Others attach themselves to other emotions, such as guilt attaching itself to shame.

Sometimes we become angry when the real underlying emotion is shame or sadness. Often one emotion will mask another in a subconscious attempt at self-preservation. How many of us can relate to outbursts of uncontrolled anger one minute, only to find ourselves sobbing with grief the next? How many of us grew up in a world where it was OK to get angry, but displaying grief was a sign of weakness? We have all heard it said, "Big boys don't cry." The truth is that boys who grow up learning that it is not OK to cry grow up to be emotionally handicapped and unavailable.

Learning to understand and untangle our emotions is vital to our recovery. As we begin this process of self-discovery, it is vital that we learn to be honest with ourselves and with others no matter how much it hurts. This is a drum that you will hear me beat throughout this book. As impossible as it may seem, we must learn to become completely transparent with what we are feeling. I encourage you to take this one step at a time. I also encourage you to find a good counselor who deals with post-traumatic stress. Hang in there; you'll get through this. One day you will look back and realize things weren't nearly as bad as you once believed.

The first step in understanding your emotions is to identify your triggers. Triggers are issues or circumstances that cause us to become emotionally charged or to want to hurt ourselves. What do I mean by "hurt ourselves"? We need to start looking at self-medication (our addiction) for what it is—we are hurting ourselves in an attempt to feel better. This is irrational because we are not thinking clearly. Self-medicating is a false road of hope. Our goal is to enter the life that God created for us to enjoy. Drugs, alcohol, and pornography lead us down a road away from that life.

The following paragraph is from *The PTSD Workbook* by Dr. Mary Beth Williams and Dr. Soili Poijula. This book is an excellent resource for helping you deal with your emotions.

> Learning to deal with what happened to you means learning to tolerate painful emotions without needing to hurt yourself or trying to avoid them totally. Some of the emotions that get associated with trauma are grief, guilt, anger, shame, and fear. Probably the hardest emotion to deal with is trigger-based fear. Again, identifying your triggers and then working on ways to take away their power is a very important way to give you a sense of control.[1]

As you learn to identify your triggers—the emotions associated with a desire to self-medicate—you need to learn how to refrain from such behavior. As I discussed in chapter three, many of these triggers can cause dissociation. If we continually medicate our emotions, we will never be able to recognize them for what they are.

For most of my life, my triggers were like landmines that I would step on before I knew they were there. For example, I would be watching a newscast or be having a conversation with someone and begin to feel anxious or sad. Soon I would start weeping or become angry. Before I made the decision to get better, without understanding what I was doing or why, I would typically reach for alcohol or watch pornography to comfort myself. The only way I understood how to deal with negative emotions was to try to numb my mind in an attempt to get them to

---

[1] Mary Beth Williams & Soili Poijula, *The PTSD Workbook: Simple, Effective Techniques for Overcoming Traumatic Stress Symptoms* (Oakland, CA: New Harbinger, 2016), 106.

go away. Most often I had no idea what was happening. All I understood was that I was upset, anxious, or angry. Either that or I would have a sense that I have often heard described as an overwhelming feeling of impending doom or grief, much of the time with no idea why.

In the last chapter I discussed the importance of staying within our window of tolerance concerning our emotions. This is difficult if not impossible if we don't begin the difficult work of self-discovery.

A big part of recovery is getting to know ourselves both emotionally and physically. Getting to know myself has been one of the most intriguing aspects of recovery. I was forty-three years old and thought I knew myself pretty well. After all, I had lived with myself for over four decades. The human mind is an amazing instrument whose primary purpose is to protect us. Our minds have an incredible ability to hide the truth from us when it deems that that truth is more than we can handle. As a result, many people go through life never quite knowing the truth.

How do we begin sorting through our emotions? By taking things one day at a time. If that's too much, start moment by moment. If you start feeling anxious or sad, stop and consider what's happening. Practice self-talk. Ask yourself what happened or why you're feeling this way. Once you identify the source, you can tell yourself, although the situation may be sad or angering, "It will be OK, and this is not worth making things worse by derailing the situation or hurting myself by self-medicating." You can also say, "I will no longer let other things or people control my emotions."

Once you learn to put this into practice (along with the help of a therapist), as time goes by, facing your emotions will become easier. You will likely begin to notice a separation between your emotional response and your physical response. Oh yes, these triggers are not just in your head. Your body has learned to respond. Once you learn not to let your emotions get the best of you, you will begin to learn to feel your body. One day you will find that you can feel your stress hormones release and your blood pressure elevate as a result of a trigger.

Your mind is a powerful tool, and it is important for you to learn to recognize what your body is trying to communicate. Most often when we begin to feel uncomfortable, the remedy is to take a pill or some other type of medication. Unfortunately, this often cuts the line of communication between the body and mind.

The Cords of Pride and Shame

As a sexual abuse victim, one of my most difficult issues is being unable to share my emotions with others or to be honest with myself due to shame. All traumatic stress has the propensity for shame, but sexual abuse survivors are often left dealing with shame in a different dynamic.

The cord of shame is complex and is often paired with pride. Many within the Church say that pride has no place in the life of a Christian. I spent years advocating this position, and I am so grateful that we are not held responsible for all the foolish things we have believed in the past. Pride is an essential part of our conscience, as intended by our Creator.

Pride can also be one of the most dangerous weapons used against us by our enemy if not understood and exercised as God intended. There is a more debilitating weapon—the blade of shame. Shame is also an important part of living as intended by our Creator. Pride and shame are weapons in the hands of our enemy that are often wielded with the same stroke. They are inseparable in many instances, two sides of the same blade.

Pride and shame are an inescapable part of our humanity. God created us in His image and likeness. From the beginning, God exhibited His pride in creation: "And God saw that the light was good" (Genesis 1:4). God was pleased with the work of His own hands. Pride gives us the sense that we are doing well. It is that little spark inside every one of us that turns up the corner of our mouths when we fix something that was broken, help a friend, or receive an "attaboy" from our boss.

Conversely, shame can be associated with frustration when we are unable to fix something, when we fail to help a friend in need, or are criticized at work for not doing something as well as we know we could have. Shame comes in many different forms, shapes, and sizes. For most of my life I equated feelings of shame with anger.

These are all healthy examples of pride and shame, but what about unhealthy pride and shame? One way we can think of unhealthy pride is pride that elevates us, in our minds above others, such as when we say to ourselves "I'm the best ballplayer on my team," or "I'm the prettiest or most handsome person in my school or at work." Unhealthy pride and shame can provoke (or expose) unhealthy shame in another. Here is a short story to illustrate one of the ways in which this happens.

Johnny goes to the store and purchases a pair of red shoes that he thinks look cool. He feels that everyone at school will think he's cool because of his new shoes. The next day as soon as Johnny walks into school, Jimmy sees Johnny's new shoes and thinks they're cool but is overcome with jealousy, thinking that all the other kids will like Johnny's shoes better than his. Jimmy quickly devises a plan to protect his self-perceived "coolest kid in school" status, and starts pointing out Johnny's shoes to everyone in the hallway. "Take a look at those shoes! Where did you get those—out of your grandfather's closet? Maybe we should take up a collection, so Johnny doesn't need to shop out of a trash can." Feeling ashamed, Johnny runs out of the front doors of the school and all the way home, throws his new shoes in the trash, and vows never to wear red shoes again. He suffers from PTRSD. (post-traumatic red shoe disorder) for the rest of his life.

Jimmy didn't create the pride that resulted in Johnny's shame. It was already part of Johnny's emotional makeup. It is part of who we are—the way God created us. As children, most of us are not mature enough or experienced enough in life to have developed healthy adult emotions. Sometimes we would witness this type of behavior amongst adults. Most would identify it as juvenile. This is another reason why child abuse is so devastating.

Children who are abused all too often become emotionally handicapped because they lack the capacity to process feelings of shame. Sometimes these handicaps are not overcome over the course of a lifetime. I suffered an emotional handicap for years, well into adulthood, becoming angry or overwhelmed with anxiety by situations that most adults would move past quickly.

Most healthy, well-adjusted people have aspects of their life of which they are proud. I am very proud of my children. Parents should be proud of their children. I have five children, and let me assure you, they have done things of which I am not proud. Yes, that means I have been ashamed of their behavior. Just as my behavior, without a doubt, has provoked my mother and father to shame. I have done some stupid things in my life.

The fact that I have been ashamed of my children's behavior does not mean I have ever been ashamed of them as people. Is there anything that my children could do to make me ashamed of them? No! The difficult thing about shame is our inability to differentiate between who a person is and the shameful things people do. God created us in His own image and likeness. He never forgets who we are.

Let's take a look at an example of how God deals with the shameful acts of His first children on earth. This is also another example of how one person's pride can affect another in shame, though it's different from our first example.

> Now the serpent was more subtle than any other wild creature that the LORD God had made. He said to the woman, "Did God say, 'You shall not eat of any tree of the garden'?"
>
> And the woman said to the serpent, "We may eat of the fruit of the trees of the garden; but God said, 'You shall not eat of the fruit of the tree which is in the midst of the garden, neither shall you touch it, lest you die.'"
>
> But the serpent said to the woman, "You will not die. For God knows that when you eat of it your eyes will be opened, and you will be like God, knowing good and evil."
>
> So when the woman saw that the tree was good for food, and that it was a delight to the eyes, and that the tree was to be desired to make one wise, she took of its fruit and ate; and she also gave some to her husband, and he ate.
>
> Then the eyes of both were opened, and they knew that they were naked; and they sewed fig leaves together and made themselves aprons.
>
> And they heard the sound of the LORD God walking in the garden in the cool of the day, and the man and his wife hid themselves from the presence of the LORD God among the trees of the garden. (Genesis 3:1–8)

The serpent, also understood to be the devil, tempted

Eve by appealing to the pride that he knew dwelt deep within her. We must never forget that our enemy is not only evil but also intelligent. He is not merely out to hurt us; his goal is to separate us from our intended home with our Lord. The serpent planted seeds of distrust in Eve's heart, "For God knows that when you eat of it your eyes will be opened, and you will be like God, knowing good and evil." Eve's heart became filled with pride and jealousy. Was this pride something that Eve had to learn? Of course not; it was part of her emotional DNA. Eve, who was completely innocent, was up against the most cunning deceivers who ever walked this planet. He is also known as the father of lies (John 8:44).

Consumed with pride, Eve ate the fruit of the Tree of the Knowledge of Good and Evil in the hope of being like God, and then she gave it to Adam, and he ate. Their eyes were opened, but instead of being like God, they understood that what they had done was sinful. Their innocence was gone, as they stood naked and full of shame for what they had done. Pride became shame.

Here is what we must understand about shame: it can never be undone. Those who walk this earth without shame for acts of sin that they have committed are mentally ill. Many who suffer from this type of illness are called sociopaths, people who are so mentally disfigured that they are incapable of feeling healthy human emotions.

Notice that Adam and Eve stitched fig leaves together to cover their nakedness. As we read a little further, we learn that, in His unceasing love and compassion, God came and clothed Adam and Eve in garments of skin (Genesis 3:21). This is important in understanding how God heals our shame. Shame is never removed; it is covered with compassion. The clothes that God made for Adam and Eve are a foreshadowing of our Lord Jesus Christ, who would cover our shame with His compassion.

I understand that you may not be touched in any way by the notion that the compassion of Jesus covers our sin and shame. When we are violated by trauma, whether it be at the hands of another or by some freak accident, part of us seeks help from deep within. When a child is abused or molested, something deep within that child cries out for an advocate.

That child may not understand what is going on with his or her emotions, but the cry goes out just the same. Likewise, the victim of a traumatic accident is often bewildered at the fact that what has happened has actually happened to them. "Where was my help?" they wonder. "Where was my advocate?" Again the question is asked deep within, even if the soul asking the question is unaware of his or her longings. Scripture says unfulfilled hope is toxic: "Hope deferred makes the heart sick, but a desire fulfilled is a tree of life"(Proverbs 13:12).

We are all created in the image of God (Genesis 1:27). Life on Earth began through a divine spark, which ignited a flame that burns to this day. Part of every human being longs to be accepted by our Creator. The shame of sin and trauma all but severs our union with God. We carry shame if we commit a sin and all too often when sin has been committed against us. Why does shame distance us from God? Some say it's because God is perfect and cannot stand in the presence of sin. This is true but not as some may believe.

God is perfect and good and cannot stand in the presence of sin by His very nature. Remember that Scripture says that we are created in God's image and likeness (Genesis 1:26–27). If we are created in God's image, and if God cannot stand in the presence of sin, we cannot stand in the presence of sin either. Sin and the ravages of shame sicken and destroy our bodies, minds, and souls and eventually lead to death, as I have discussed throughout this book.

Shame sickens our beings, and we often medicate the pain even if we have no idea what we are doing or why. We were created to be fully alive and walk in peace and love with our Creator. When we sin, we hide from God in shame just like Adam and Eve hid in the Garden. Look at what happened there. God came looking for them. They were hiding in shame, but God sought them out. Can God stand in the presence of sin? Of course He can! He stood in the Garden with Adam and Eve just as Jesus ate and drank with sinners (Matthew 11:19).

God can physically stand in the presence of sin, but it goes against His nature, which is full of compassion, to see His sons and daughters ravaged by the poison of shame. He is not only holy and just; He is compassionate beyond understanding.

Here is a fictional narrative to help you understand.

> God reached through the thicket in which Adam and Eve were hiding and turned their faces toward His. "Look at me," He said. Their eyes diverted away. Again He said, "Look at me." They looked up at God, lost in shame. "I love you, and I always will," He said. "What the two of you did was not OK in any way, but we are going to get through this. I am here with you, and I always will be."

God did not take away their shame. He covered it with His love through His compassion. Love conquers all. God began Adam and Eve's long healing process (which represents all of humanity). Now reflecting upon what we have just read, let us reconsider the statement that "God cannot stand in the presence of sin." Yes, it is true but not for the reasons some may espouse. Because of His infinite compassion and His very nature, it breaks His heart to see His children suffer.

The Cord of Guilt

The difficult aspect of the cord of guilt is that it attaches itself to the cord of shame and is associated with pride. Like our other emotions, guilt is a vital part of our conscience, but it can become a festering wound. Guilt is the part of our emotions that helps us understand we have done something wrong.

Guilt comes about as the result of shame and can be referred to as feeling ashamed; they are one and the same. There is a difference between shame and guilt though (feeling ashamed). Once we begin to understand this, healing can begin. Shame leaves scars, but guilt (feeling ashamed) is a festering wound. The only way that guilt can be healed is through forgiveness. It has been said that "time heals all wounds." This may be true of broken hearts, but time can't fix the guilt of shame. Time allows the wound of guilt to fester until, like a poison, it sickens and destroys the life of the one who consumes it. I spent years replacing the feeling of guilt with anger because of pride.

Rabbit Trail

Emotions are complex and far beyond our understanding. Countless books have been written on the subject of human psychology. All it takes is a trip to Barnes and Noble or an Internet search, to become overwhelmed by the seemingly limitless number of opinions as to why humans act as they do. I certainly don't have all the answers. As I mentioned above, I wrote this chapter to help gain a better understanding of our emotions as they per-tain to healing from the pain of abuse.

The English language is limited as to how we express certain concepts or ideas. Shame is one of those concepts. The word "shame" is too wide of a brush to effectively communicate all the emotions that this one small word implies. We could have used many words to communicate the many emotions involved with shame.

Please bear with me as I venture to express what I have learned about dealing with the pain, shame, and guilt of past trauma. Much of what I am discussing this book will plant seeds in your heart. I have often read a book or had something communicated through a counselor that has taken months or even years to take hold and mature in my heart. God often works this way. Jesus describes the word of God as a seed when explaining the parable of the sower to his disciples (Luke 8:11).

Back to the point:

Forgiveness is vitally important to recovery, but all too often it's a place where we get stuck. It's important to understand that there are two different types of shame and guilt. One type of shame and guilt is legitimate and can only be reconciled through forgiveness and compassion. The other type of shame and guilt is impossible to reconcile because it is not legitimately ours, as I touched on in chapter six when I discussed codependency.

Shame has no influence on God's love for us. God did not love Adam and Eve any less after they ate the forbidden fruit. Nor should shame affect the love one person has for another, but all too often it does. Love tends to become buried beneath a mountain of misplaced emotions.

My uncle abused me when I was a toddler. I have no memory of what happened, but I still feel shame. I have never felt responsible for the situation, but it has made me feel fatally broken or tarnished and for a time, angry. Words cannot describe the way I felt. What my uncle did to me was not my fault in any way, but it was still shameful. It was shameful for me, being the victim, and it was shameful for my uncle. This awful event will always be shameful. I assume my uncle felt shame for molesting a child who just so happened to be me.

I have forgiven my uncle, and I hope my uncle has forgiven himself, but a thousand years from now, if someone asks him if he regrets molesting me, the answer will undoubtedly be *yes*. The shame will never go away, but I love him just the same. If I am asked a thousand years from now if I regret the situation, I will undoubtedly say *yes*. It changed the course of my entire life, and the shame never goes away, but I love myself just the same. We can only control our own emotions, and I have chosen love.

I will always wonder what could have gone so awfully wrong in my uncle's life—this man who loved our Lord—that caused him to molest a child. Was he molested as a child? I may never know, and that's OK. I love my uncle just the same. Suffering gives birth to compassion. If sin had not entered the world, there would have been no need for Christ to enter the world. There would have been no need for the cross.

A phrase often used in the Catholic Church's Latin mass speaks to this understanding: "*O felix culpa quae talem et tantum meruit habere redemptorem.*" This means "O happy fault (sin) which received as its reward so great and so good a redeemer." This beautiful sentiment expresses gratefulness that sin came into the world, allowing humankind to experience God's loving grace through the person of Jesus Christ. Literature, art, and music throughout the ages is rich with this sentiment in the paradigm of human love—tragedy or misfortune giving way to an encounter with love or fortune which would not have been possible any other way.

It was Adam and Eve's shame that caused God, in His unyielding love and compassion, to make skins to cover their nakedness. I know it would have been better if I had never been molested, but as hard as it may be to understand, that shameful act has given birth to compassion, though only after a long, painful gestation.

Compassion

> Thus the authority of compassion is the possibility of man to forgive his brother, because forgiveness is only real for him who has discovered the weakness of his friends and the sins of his enemy in his own heart and is willing to call every human being his brother.[2]
>
> —Henrie J.M. Nouwen, *The Wounded Healer*

Compassion is not feeling sorry for someone. That emotion is better defined as sympathy. Compassion goes much deeper. Compassion is something that we share with someone. I don't know that I could have felt compassion for my abusers without experiencing my own shame. I understand that some may be wondering how I could even begin to have compassion for those who treated me in such a way. It's because I realize blame does not heal. Blame reinforces the cords of pride and anger, which strengthens shame. Blame does nothing more than hinder healing and destroy love. I stood for years with my hands held firmly on my hips and my jaw locked in the resolve never to forgive. I deceived myself, my shame masked by anger.

I am not sure which occurred first, compassion for

---

[2] Henry J. M. Nouwen, *The Wounded Healer: Ministry in Contemporary Society* (New York, NY: Doubleday, 1972), 41.

myself or my abusers, but as I began to deal with my emotions, the image of compassion started to take shape through the fog of my past. Once I learned to stop the blame and anger, compassion for others began taking hold in my life, and the strangest thing started to happen. The healing began. I not only started forgiving others; I started forgiving myself.

The word of God tells us that we are to "put on" compassion (Colossians 3:12). Compassion is something that is supposed to come alive in a Christian's life. I believe compassion exists in the hearts of all people but is kept hidden away and anesthetized by our false selves.

Compassion struggles to make itself known when we see someone passed out on the street corner strung out on drugs, when we read about a heinous crime or murder, or when we turn on the television and see a story about a prostitute being arrested. Compassion is that little part of us that wonders what could have gone so wrong in these people's lives. It is the stirring of our true self that understands that it could be us lying on the street corner, with our story in the paper or on the six o'clock news.

Compassion is given life when we begin to understand that our desperate need for love is not unique but shared with all of humanity and the selfish act of abuse that we have suffered is no less cruel than that which we harbor in our own hearts. Compassion takes its first breath when we recognize the bitterness and anger of the world as our own and when tears of joy take us by surprise as we witness an act of kindness—exposing the authentic heart of our inner person. Compassion becomes fully alive when we recognize ourselves in all people.

We begin to walk in the power of the cross not when we are forgiven but when we walk in the authority of compassion and forgiveness (Matthew 6:15). We share in Christ's suffering when we offer aid and comfort and to those who have spit in our faces (Matthew 26:67). We become children of our Father in Heaven when we lift up in prayer those who have abused and despitefully used us (Matthew 5:44).

I would like to end this chapter with the words of Beverly Engle, taken from a *Psychology Today* article titled, "How Compassion Can Heal Shame from Childhood: The Antidote to Shame." The quote at the beginning of this chapter comes from the same piece.

> Compassion comes from the Latin roots com (with) and pati (suffer), or to "suffer with." When we offer genuine compassion, we join a person in his or her suffering. Self-compassion then, begins with connecting with one's own suffering. Unfortunately, most of us don't want to do this. We want to forget about our past suffering and put it behind us. By doing so, however, we don't heal the emotions that accompany the suffering—the pain, fear, anger, and especially, the shame. The same holds true for painful and shaming experiences in the present. Instead of stopping to acknowledge our suffering in the moment, we try to move past it as soon as possible.
>
> Self-compassion encourages us to begin to treat ourselves and talk to ourselves with the same kindness, caring and compassion we would show a good friend or a beloved child. In addition, it helps us to feel less isolated and alienated from others. The more shame we feel, the more deficient we feel and in turn, the more separate we feel from others. But self-compassion helps us to recognize our common humanity—the fact that we have all done things that we feel ashamed about and that we all ex-

perience the same pain in difficult times.[3]

---

[3] Beverly Engle, "How Compassion Can Heal Shame from Childhood: The Antidote to Shame," Psychology Today, July 14, 2013, https://www.psychologytoday.com/us/blog/the-compassion-chronicles/201307/how-compassion-can-heal-shame-childhood

Chapter 13

The Path Toward Healing

"It's not the destination, it's the journey."

—Ralph Waldo Emerson, *Self-Reliance*

How can you restore balance to your life? Some people have no idea what it's like to exist without the memories of trauma or the constant undulation of living between hyper- or hypoarousal—the roller-coaster ride of overreacting or being numb to life's circumstances. How can you stop your past from dictating how you react to your present-day life? How can you become fully alive to the here and now? How can you find freedom from an existence that is all you have ever known?

As we move along in search for the answers to these questions it is important for us to understand one thing about our journey toward healing—the path is the destination. As long as we are on the path, we have arrived. Many will ask, "How long will it take for me to be healed?" There is no answer to this question on this side of Heaven. I have been walking on the path for twelve years now. I am nowhere near where I hope to be one day, but I am so much better than when I started. You see, I am not writing this as one who has arrived but as a fellow sojourner. This book is about helping my fellow travelers along the way.

One of my goals in life is to hike the Appalachian Trail (AT). The AT is a thin 2,190-mile path that runs between

Springer Mountain in Georgia and Mount Katahdin in Maine. Every spring, hundreds of people find their way to one of these two locations and attempt to hike the entire trail. These folks are referred to as "thru hikers" amongst those of us in the Appalachian Trail community. I am what is referred to as a "section hiker." My plan is to tackle the trail by hiking one small section at a time, year after year until I complete the trail. A common phrase used by those in the community that has become somewhat of a mantra is "Hike your own hike." We all hike the same thin green corridor, but comparing yourself to another hiker will do nothing more than take the joy out of your journey. It can be frustrating trying to keep up with another hiker, and it is equally frustrating having to continually slow down to allow someone to catch up.

Many who hike the trail in a group begin each day by designating a location to camp that night. Then everyone in the group hikes at their own pace and meets at the designated location. We are all walking the same trail, but we are all different. For the most part, any of us in the community will do whatever we can to help another hiker, but the hard work is up to each one of us individually. The path toward healing is much the same. All of us have been affected by the ups and downs of this life. Nobody escapes untouched by trauma. All of us need time to heal—some more than others—but we are not part of some cosmic competition. We are all part of the same human family. The early Church adopted the name "The Way" (Acts 9:2). They understood that none of us will "arrive" during this life.

Hundreds if not thousands of books have been written about healing from trauma. Please do not let this book or any other book take the place of counseling. Please go and find someone who specializes in PTSD and grief counseling, and begin the journey. A book will never replace human interaction.

The first step toward healing is learning to trust. I strongly encourage you not to begin this journey with a family member or even a pastor or a close family friend. Often the familiarity inherent in such relationships can add confusion to an already delicate situation. Abuse survivors often have some tense and potentially explosive emotions hovering just beneath the surface of their awareness. It is much better to be in the presence of someone who expects and understands how to deal with these emotions as they surface. The way these emotions are dealt with can make all the difference in how we heal.

On *Childhood Disrupted*, Donna Jackson Nakazawa says,

> When you are in a therapeutic relationship with a skilled therapist and experience something "old," that memory is paired with the positive experience of being seen by someone who attunes to you, sees you, and accepts you just as you are, whatever your experience was—and you begin to heal. When you begin to feel trust, perhaps for the first time in your life, and when this process is repeated, you modify old circuits in the brain that tell you that you cannot trust. You create new brain cells and connections that allow you to create new habits and responses to other people. Indeed, part of the power of therapy is that one can learn, finally, as an adult, to become attached to a safe person. You can begin to feel safe in engaging, interacting, and bonding in a relationship. In this way, a therapist's unconditional acceptance rewires you so that you have a more fully formed, healthier sense of self.[1]

---

[1] Donna Jackson Nakazawa, *Childhood Disrupted: How Your Biography Becomes Your Biology, and How You Can Heal* (New York, NY: Atria, 2015), 187.

I am not a pastor or a licensed counselor, but I have been walking this path for many years. As I wind up this book, there are four things that I would like to impart to you as you hike your own hike of healing. Think of these as guideposts or trail markers along the way.

1. Breaking the Silence

Your healing path begins by breaking the silence. Think of it as the trailhead—your first trail marker.

At age forty-three, I was overcome with the overwhelming desire to push back against the darkness of my past. At that time I had no idea about recovery or the mountain I was about to climb. All I knew was something was trapped within me that needed to come out.

As Dr. van der Kolk says,

> Activists in the early campaign for AIDS awareness created a powerful slogan: "Silence = Death." Silence about trauma also leads to death—the death of the soul. Silence reinforces the godforsaken isolation of trauma. Being able to say aloud to another human being, "I was raped" or "I was battered by my husband" or "My parents called it discipline, but it was abuse" or "I'm not making it since I got back from Iraq," is a sign that healing can begin.[2]

There is something powerful about looking in the eyes of another human being sharing your deepest pain, and receiving in return, through the look in their eyes and the affirmation of their lips, that regardless of what has happened in your past, it is OK, and that you are loved, valua-

---

[2] Bessel van der Kolk, *The Body Keeps the Score: Brain, Mind, and Body in the Healing of Trauma* (New Your, NY: Penguin, 2015), 234.

ble, and/or forgiven. It is compassion through the human experience that most often and most effectively breaks the bonds of shame.

Here is the thing about sharing my past—my world didn't come to an end. The earth didn't quake, and nobody hated me. Through all the pain, I felt a freedom like I had never experienced. It was exciting, exhilarating, and painful beyond words all at once. It was hard, but the thing I feared most was exactly what I needed.

2. Writing

It comes. You know that It is not of yourself. It is from without, and It attaches Itself to your deepest parts. First comes loneliness, then abandonment, then despair, then the pain is so great you want It to end by any means. Just before you are crushed by the grip of It, there comes a trickle of love that can only come from the Divine. Then, It pours . . . no, It gushes in, without removing any of the pain. The volume of Its presence actually pushes the pain deeper into your being. Every cell of your body shares the pain with your heart. Your body, soul, and spirit collapse at His feet. You feel you don't have the strength to lift your fingers. Like discovering that you are in the middle of the ocean and realizing that you are standing on an inch of ice, without any earthly hope, a small part of you wishes it would break, while the rest of you is trying not to move, so you can stay alive. The ends of your fingers actually tingle with expectation. Now you wish without repentance that Whatever has entered your being would crush you and drag you back with It. You never want It to leave. Now It subsides, you feel It pulling away, and you grab for It in desperation. But there is nothing you can do to hang onto It. You cannot control It's coming, or It's going. You just know that you will spend the rest of your life longing for It above all else. You will never be the same. Then you realize, when It left, It took with It every bit of anger, shame, and resentment from who you are, because It has captured your heart. You want the whole world to have It—but It is not yours to give."

I wrote this in the weeks after I broke the silence about my abuse. I needed to put words to what I was experiencing. The emotions and bodily feelings were so "other than" anything I had ever experienced. I could feel God's touch through the confusion.

This was when I learned how much God truly loves me. God loves me so much that He was unwilling to allow me to continue to stuff down any more of the pain. He was not concerned about disrupting my life. The only thing He was concerned with was getting me well no matter how much it hurt. He feels the same way about all of His children. I think of it like going through chemotherapy. He would administer the healing touch of His Holy Spirit, knowing it would be excruciating. He did not take away the pain that He knew was necessary, but He was right by my side, rubbing my back and comforting me during the process. As odd as this may sound, the sweetness of His touch was worth all the agony.

Something about writing purges the soul. It draws out desires and yearnings that have longed to give voice but have remained trapped in dark caverns of fear. The words above were the first of countless that I have written over the past twelve years. At times it is as if my fingers have a mind of their own as I watch words that I never knew I had within me a scroll across my laptop's screen.

For me, writing has been about two things. First, it has allowed me to learn things about myself—my feelings and emotions—that I don't know that I would have learned any other way. Something about seeing your thoughts and feelings in writing provokes honesty. When I see what I am feeling expressed in words, I want them to be authentic. Writing gives me time to reflect upon my deepest feelings and motives. Most of what I write is just for me, written in the privacy of my office, or tucked away in some quiet corner of wherever I am. Yes, I share some of what I write with others, but I get to decide what and when.

This book is composed of bits and pieces of what I have written on the subject of my recovery and trauma over the past twelve years. If I were to share it all, it would require volumes. Much of what I have written, I haven't shown to anybody, and there are other things that I have only shown to my therapist or close friends.

The second reason I have found so much joy in writing is that it allows me to express myself. Writing allows us to collect our thoughts and express ourselves on our own terms and in our own time. How many of us have walked away from conversation only to realize we neglected to communicate something we had intended, or even worse, said too much?

You may be thinking, "Writing may be good for you, but I'm not a good writer." Self-confidence is something that I have struggled with my entire life. Writing has been extremely difficult for me. I have dyslexia and am probably one of the worst spellers on the planet. That paragraph that you read at the beginning of this section only reads the way it does because of the help of a close friend, several proofreaders, and two editors. The first draft was awkward and filled with hardly decipherable misspelled words and punctuation. If it had been expressed in the spoken word, it would have been nothing more than guttural utterances.

I encourage you to pick up a pen and paper or a laptop and start writing. Carve out a time every day just for you and your writing. For me, morning works best while the house is quiet, and I can be alone with my thoughts. I wake up, grab a glass of water, and head up to my office where I begin my day by reading a couple of chapters of the Bible, spending some time in meditation and prayer, and then writing.

Write about your past. Write about your abuse and how you feel. Whatever you do, don't worry about using eloquent words, spelling, or punctuation—just write. You are writing for yourself, and at times perhaps for God, but He is not interested in how well you write. He is interested in what's in your heart. If you are hurting, write about your pain. If you are happy, write about that. If you are pissed off at God, put it down in words. God is tough. You won't be the first to be mad at God, and you certainly won't be the last. The point is that you need to write exactly what you are feeling and thinking. Your feelings are important. It's time to start treating them as such. Some of the things you write may be uncomfortable, but that's OK. No one will ever read what you have written unless you choose to share it with somebody.

I'll conclude this point by quoting Donna Jackson Nakazawa: "Studies show that writing about stressful experiences not only helps patients to get better, it keeps them from getting worse."[3]

---

[3] Nakazawa, *Childhood Disrupted,* 187.

3. Mindfulness & Yoga

As I consider the trauma and abuse of my childhood I realize that above all I regret what it has stolen from me—all of the wasted years of being stuck in my past and paralyzed with anxiety about the future. As we discussed in chapter nine, for many of us it is not the trauma itself that disrupts our lives, but the way it has caused us to view and react to life and world around us. Hyper- and hypovigilance doesn't steel our lives all at once like death, but instead, one day, one minute, and one moment at a time. If we are not careful, before we are aware of what has happened, we may find that our lives have slipped away without our ever really learning to live.

What the practice of mindfulness and yoga has done for me is help me to begin to live in those moments that were once wasted. It has helped me begin to "regain" a sense of the future. It has also helped me to experience physical feelings and emotions for what they are instead of being clouded by the haze of dissociation. I use the word "regain" as if this sense of life is something that I remember. The truth is that it is all together new to me. I am learning to enjoy each day as the gift that it was meant to be by our Creator. I am slowly gaining a sense of the future and experiencing feelings and emotions in whole new way. I still have times when I allow the preciouses moments of this life to be stolen by the trauma of my past, but just the fact that I recognize what is happening is monumental.

The purpose of this section is to share with the reader the benefits that I have received through mindfulness and yoga. However, it is my experience that that mindfulness and yoga are most effective when implemented with other forms of therapy. I have found that the most affective approach toward the healing of trauma is holistic and as I have mentioned many times throughout this book is best achieved with guidance of a competent mental health professional. There are many good avenues of healing available to us, some of which we have discussed in this book, along with many others we have not. This as why it is so important to seek guidance in choosing the best approach. All of us that have suffered trauma share in the fact that our lives have been painfully altered by our experiences, but most of our stories are a little deferent, and will most likely require attention that is unique to our individual needs.

I understand that many within the Christian community view both mindfulness and yoga as part of the New Age movement. Let me assure you that this understanding couldn't be further from the truth. There is inarguably a growing trend among those involved in New Age spirituality to claim both mindfulness and yoga as their own, just as some of these groups claim Christianity. The religious aspects of mindfulness and yoga are incompatible with Christianity, but they are not inherently part of New Age spirituality.

Let me make it perfectly clear that when I advocate the practice mindfulness that I am promoting the practical application and am not encouraging anyone to practice Buddhism or any other eastern religion—not that Buddhism is wrong or bad. I have the deepest respect for those who follow the way of the Buddha. Buddhism and yoga are both ancient practices developed and practiced by people who desire to live at peace with themselves and the world around them. Both practices originated in India. The founder of Buddhism, Siddhartha Gautama, lived during the fifth century BC,[4] and evidence of the practice

---

[4] "Buddhism," *History*, Jul. 22, 2020, https://www.history.com/topics/religion/buddhism.

of yoga dates to as early as 2,700 BC.[5] Those involved in the development of these practices had no concept of Christ, nor was either developed as an affront to Christianity.

I have read numerous books and articles that attempt to reconcile Christianity and Buddhism. As hard as we may try, it is impossible to fit a round peg into a square hole without disfiguring one or the other. One cannot be a Christian and a Buddhist, as some claim to be possible. This does not mean we cannot recognize the good in a life of mindfulness. It is entirely possible to live mindfully in Christ.

Let us begin by learning how breathing properly, which can help in reducing stress and in regulation your autonomic nervous system as I discussed in chapter four. When you inhale you activate the sympathetic nervous system, which increases your heart rate through the release of hormones. When you exhale you activate the parasympathetic nervous system, which lowers your heart rate through the vagus nerve. One way to calm your body, mind, and nervous system is by learning to breathe properly.[6]

An effective way of reducing stress is deep breathing. Take a deep breath in, preferably by extending the abdomen. Then slowly let it out by pulling in the abdomen. Inhale deep and slow, and exhale even slower. Think of it as taking twice as long or longer to exhale than to inhale. For example, if you breathe in for five seconds, exhale for ten seconds. Make adjustments for whatever is comfortable. You may need to start off with shorter breaths or purse your lips on exhalation to help with regulation.

Most have heard someone say, "Just relax and take a

---

[5] Dr. Ishwar V. Basavaraddi, "Yoga: Its Origin, History and Development," *Ministry of External Affairs, Government of India*, April 23, 2015, https://www.mea.gov.in/in-focus-article.htm?25096/Yoga+Its+Origin+History+and+Development
[6] van der Kolk, *The Body Keeps Score*, 79.

few deep breaths." Well, the next time you're feeling stressed, do exactly that. I was amazed at how much it helped when I first learned this simple technique. The great thing is that you can do it just about anywhere and at any time without drawing attention to yourself. You can do it while you're in traffic or even when you're with your kids or your boss is bungee jumping on your last nerve. They don't even need to know what you're doing. Just quietly inhale slowly and exhale even slower.

You can use this type of breathing to time how long you hold your positions during yoga. If you would like to hold a position for a minute or two, deep breathe for as many cycles as required. You can make adjustments, so it fits your routine. During my yoga practice, I begin by exhaling from deep in my lower abdomen and keep pushing all the way up to my mouth until I have nothing left to push, and then I hold for a few more seconds. Picture yourself squeezing a tube of toothpaste from the bottom and working your way to the top until the tube is completely empty.

I practice what I call "yoga-es," which is a series of yoga postures mixed with stretching exercises that somewhat resembles the movements of Tai Chi in that I focus on flexing and opening my hips and joints. This came about as I sought ways to reduce stress in my abdomen, lower back, and hips. Yoga can be practiced in the privacy of your own home or with others.

Countless apps and publications are available to help in these practices, and yoga classes are offered in most communities. However, as you begin your practice, you may desire to start at home, especially if you have a history of abuse. I was surprised by, and somewhat unprepared for, some of the bodily sensations and emotions that occurred during some of the positions. Again, I strongly encourage you to find a grief and trauma counselor as you begin your recovery efforts.

I am going to leave the subject of yoga, and focus on the subject of mindfulness. As I discussed above, mindfulness also comes with some misconceptions, especially for those of us in the Christian community. Please hang in there with me as I attempt to clear up some of them.

When most of us think of mindfulness, we think of meditation, but it is so much more. Meditation is just one part of mindfulness. Mindfulness meditation is also referred to as "sitting practice."[7] Sitting practice is not prayer or a path to enlightenment. For those of us healing from trauma, this practice is nothing more than a way to exercise the mind—a way of teaching your mind to be fully present in and alive to the moment.

Begin by finding a quiet place to relax for five to twenty minutes or longer if desired. Find a comfortable position—not too comfortable, though. You don't want to fall asleep. Many purists feel that getting in just the right position is paramount. Countless books cover the subject of the proper position. This is not something that I get too hung up on though. Simply sit cross-legged on the floor, in a comfortable chair, on the edge of your bed, or even in your car. I have spent plenty of time meditating in my car.

Once you achieve a good physical position, it's time to focus. Keep the word "focus" in mind. The idea is not to think of nothing but to keep your mind focused while at the same time quiet and at rest. Jon Kabat-Zinn refers to this state of mind as "non-doing."[8]

Christian meditation is similar but different regarding one's focus and "non-doing." The Church has an old and established practice of meditation that focuses on God and His kingdom, but this is not that practice, and that's

---

[7] John Kabat-Zinn, *Full Catastrophe Living: Using the Wisdom of Your Body and Mind to Face Stress, Pain, and Illness* (New York: Bantam, 2015), 141.
[8] Ibid, 26.

OK. I will discuss Christian meditation in the next section. This practice is about you. This does not mean you cannot be with God during your practice, but keep in mind that the purpose of the practice is to heal your out-of-sync cognitive processes and nervous system. Don't think of this as prayer because it's not. I will cover prayer as we move along, but for now, it is more than OK for you to focus on yourself.

Keep in mind that our Father's desire for us is that we become whole and well. His purpose for us during this life is the restoration and healing of our bodies, minds, and souls. This is what love does and who God is. He is, among many things, Jehovah Raphe, which means, "Our God Who Heals."

When I begin meditation, I close my eyes and invite Jesus to be present with me throughout my sitting practice. As you sit, you can either close your eyes or focus on something a few feet away. Either way, begin by choosing an anchor for your minds—a focal point. I prefer to close my eyes and focus on my breathing. This is not the deep breathing that I discussed above—just regular breathing.

An anchor or focal point often used in traditional sitting practice is repeating a mantra (utterance), such as the sound "om" (or AUM mantra), which is considered a universal mantra. Other short affirmations are commonly used as well, such as "I am divine love" or "Let go and let God."[9]

Whether you focus on a mantra, a short utterance, or your breathing, the idea is not to think about this action but to use it only as an anchor or focal point. This is one of the areas that significantly separates mindfulness and Christian meditation. As a Christian, to continuously speak the name of God or an attribute of His kingdom

---

[9] "What Is Mantra Meditation?", *Mindfulness.com,* last accessed Dec. 1, 2020, https://mindworks.org/blog/what-is-mantra-meditation/.

without thinking about what we are saying is to take the Lord's name in vain. Therefore, I focus on my breathing. At times I feel compelled to offer up words and thoughts of adoration to our Lord during my practice. As I mentioned above, my attitude throughout my meditation is being with Him. However, let me remind you that the purpose of this mediation is to train your mind, get to know yourself, and heal your cognitive processes and nervous system. This exercise is primarily introspective.

It is easy to lose focus because of religious guilt. I wrestled with guilt for months. Sitting in meditation felt so much like prayer that I felt like I was being unfaithful to God. Again, let me reiterate, this is not prayer. You are not seeking enlightenment but simply spending time in the practice of controlling your thoughts and learning to understand your body's sensations and emotions. You can become distracted by misplaced fear or guilt just as easily as by all the inappropriate thoughts running through your mind.

A traumatized mind will always find a reason to worry. Take away every reason, and an anxious mind will create new avenues of obsessive worrying. The cause for our uncontrolled fight-or-flight response is not the future, the past, or God but our own minds. The past is not the problem, the future is not the problem, and God is not the problem. The problem is the way we perceive, the past, our future, and God. Most of the time, God is not upset with us, but if we think He is, in our minds He becomes an angry critical being who we will never please and from whom there is no escape. Most have heard the old adage, "Perception is reality."

As we sit and focus on our breathing, the battle begins. Thoughts and concerns invade our minds. This is the primary reason why we sit and focus on our breathing. We are learning to gently let go of our thoughts. It's just that simple, or is it?[10]

As you learn to enter into mediation, you will begin to experience bodily sensations. These sensations can include, but are limited to, anxiety, sadness, joy, happiness, dread, stomach pains, pain in the head, tightness in the abdomen or back, or numbness or tingling in the legs, hands, or feet.[11] It's important to observe these sensations as invited friends.

I realize it may sound absurd to consider a headache or a numb leg as an invited friend, and I will be the first to admit to shifting position slightly to alleviate discomfort in my back from time to time. However, the goal is to reach the point where you learn to listen to your body and what it is trying to tell you. Many of us have a lifetime of experience with ignoring our body's cries for attention. However, if you are experiencing excessive pain during mediation, stop and find another position. This is not an exercise in masochism. If your discomfort becomes too painful, it will add to your stress, thus defeating the purpose of the exercise.

Another way of learning to get to know your body is through the practice of the body scan.[12] Jon Kabat-Zinn has developed an app that has been a great help to me in learning the body scan. The app is called JKZ Series1 and is available for both Apple and Android devices. The body scan is typically practiced by lying on your back and exploring your body with your mind, area by area. For example, start with the top of your head and take note of what sensation you feel in that area, if anything. From there, work down your body until you reach your toes, taking time to visit with each individual area.

The idea behind not considering what you are feeling

---

[10] Zinn, *Full Catastrophe Living*, 1–12.
[11] Ibid., 61–74.
[12] Ibid., 75–97.

as good or bad is that you are learning to become better acquainted with your body. You are learning to become better acquainted with your physical sensations and emotions. As I mentioned above, our bodies are continuously speaking, but many of us have no idea how to listen. At fifty-two years old, I discovered things about my body that I never understood. For example, I found that my body carries stress primarily in my abdomen and my lower back. For me, having tightly contracted and tense muscles in these areas felt normal.

Jon Kabat-Zinn explains the following:

> One very important domain of our lives and experience that we tend to miss, ignore, abuse, or lose control of as a result of being in the automatic pilot mode is our own body. We may be barely in touch with our body, unaware of how it is feeling most of the time. As a consequence, we can be insensitive to how our body is being affected by the environment, by our actions, and even by our thoughts and emotions. If we are unaware of these connections, we might easily feel that our body is out of control and we will have no idea why. As you will see in Chapter 21, physical symptoms are messages the body is giving us that allow us to know how it is doing and what its needs are. When we are more in touch with our body as a result of paying attention to it systematically, we will be far more attuned to what it is telling us and better equipped to respond appropriately. Learning to listen to your body is vital to improving your health and the quality of your life.
>
> Even something as simple as relaxation can be frustratingly elusive if you are unaware of your body. The stress of daily living often produces

tension that tends to localize in particular muscle groups, such as the shoulders, the jaw, and the forehead. In order to release this tension, you first have to know it is there. You have to feel it. Then you have to know how to shut off the automatic pilot and how to take over the controls of your own body and mind.[13]

Soon after learning to meditate, I realized I had no idea how to relax. I was discovering a new normal. My body had been speaking to me in many ways, undoubtedly for years, as I squelched its voice through self-medication and my mind's ability to tuck away things that it didn't want to acknowledge. As I mentioned in a previous chapter, our minds are created with a powerful defense mechanism. This mechanism will hide information that it considers too much for us to bear. As discussed in chapter three, this type of disassociation, often referred to as depersonalization or derealization, can be necessary for the survival of the traumatized mind, but not without a cost. Suppressed emotions can lead to years and often a lifetime of unexplained and misunderstood physical and mental health distress and illness.

Just as we do not consider sensations or feelings good or bad, it is important to do the same with our thoughts. We need to treat all thoughts the same and simply let them go. We should do this without judgment or concern as to whether they are good or bad. There is no good or bad during this exercise.

You will inevitably have a thought enter your mind that is lustful or morally incompatible with your beliefs. This is a judgment-free zone. When I started my practice, whenever I had such a thought, I felt ashamed and asked God to forgive me. Asking for forgiveness is a good thing.

---

[13] Ibid., 13.

However, God knows why we are meditating. He is fully aware of the battle. He understands our hearts, and I am convinced that He loves the fact that we are learning to let these thoughts go. During my frustration, I could hear Him say to me, "Stop beating yourself up and relax. I'm here with you, and we're going to get through this together."

Remember, one of our biggest stumbling blocks with shame is our perception of God. God is not sitting in Heaven with a big hammer waiting for us to screw up, so he can clobber us over the head. God loves us and is for us. (I will discuss learning to trust God in the next section.)

Through meditation we are not accepting sinful or immoral thoughts; we are letting them go. As you learn to view these thoughts as neutral guests instead of receiving them with shame, they will lose their power over your life. One of the traditional practices of mindfulness is called loving-kindness meditation.[14] The purpose of this practice is to learn to love and be kind to ourselves and the world around us without judgment—i.e., unconditional love. This is not to say we accept immoral behavior, but we stop beating ourselves up over our shortcomings and faults and become as encouraging toward ourselves as we would toward a friend or a loved one.

When we learn to treat ourselves with unconditional loving-kindness (compassion), we learn to treat those in the world around us the same way. Our Lord Jesus proclaimed in the Sermon on the Mount, "But I say to you, Love your enemies and pray for those who persecute you, so that you may be sons of your Father who is in heaven" (Matthew 5:44).

Learn to love and be kind to yourself. You are worth the effort.

---

[14] Ibid., 214–218.

Dr. Mark W. Muesse, in his teaching, *Practicing Mindfulness: An Introduction to Meditation*, produced by Great Courses, describes his own thoughts before he began the practice of mindfulness as "mindlessness"—a state of mind that I can relate to all too well.[15] Most of us go through life giving our minds free rein with very little thought as to who is running the show. Mindfulness is the practice of becoming aware of and taking control of your thoughts. Through mindfulness you are not seeking anything. You are simply becoming mindful of your thoughts and learning to become fully present in every moment.

In his second letter to the Corinthians, the Apostle Paul writes, "and every pretension raising itself against the knowledge of God, and take every thought captive in obedience to Christ, and we are ready to punish every disobedience, once your obedience is complete" (2 Corinthians 10:5–6). He is referring to his readers' own "disobedience" in allowing their thoughts to become distracted by the mindset of this world.

As we meditate the goal is to be present in the moment, not the next moment or the one that comes before but in *this* moment, the only moment that truly exists. During this moment, focus (don't think about) entirely on your breathing. Remember thoughts are not good or bad. We treat all invading thoughts the same, we just simply let them go.

At times you will have few invading thoughts. You will also have days when you will have plenty of opportunity to practice putting thoughts aside. One day is not better than the other, just different. Don't get frustrated. This is hard work. You will have days when you struggle with thoughts like "I don't have time for this today" or "What's

---

[15] Mark W. Muesse, "Practicing Mindfulness: An Introduction of Meditation," *Great Courses*, July 8, 2013, https://www.thegreatcourses.com/courses/practicing-mindfulness-an-introduction-to-meditation.html.

the use? I just can't concentrate today." Trust me when I tell you that when most begin mindfulness meditation it is anything but peaceful. However, it is well worth the struggle.

It is OK to put on a little music if that helps. I have several meditation albums in my iTunes library. My favorite source is Amazon music. I simply say, "Alexa, play meditative music," and she takes care of the rest. A little music is especially helpful to drown out distracting noises like a television playing down the hall or, as is often the case in our house, grandchildren playing.

It is also helpful to use a timer. I use my cell phone or iPad. As you are starting your practice, it is helpful to limit your meditation to short periods of time. Set your timer for five minutes. It is much easier to settle your mind when you have a goal, and that goal is only five minutes away. This will also help you make time for mindfulness during the day.

It is helpful when establishing a new discipline to break things up into smaller bites. We can often get our heads wrapped around five minutes in the morning instead of a half hour or forty-minutes. After five minutes becomes manageable, extend the time to ten minutes and so on. I seldom meditate in the morning for more than twenty minutes. I prefer to break my practice up over the course of a day. I enjoy a short sitting practice at night before bed. It makes for good sleep. I practice other types of mediation during the day, which I will get into as we move along.

The word "practice" used in the term "mindfulness practice" is not the word we use for practicing for something but rather as a learned skill or idea that we put into practice. However, it is helpful to think of meditation as practice. What are we practicing for? We are practicing for life. Mindfulness is not something we do in a quiet corner of our homes. It is a way of life. We practice while we are driving. For example, put away the cell phone and become aware of everything involved in the experience of driving to work—the cars around you and the scenery.

It's amazing when you start seeing things you never noticed before. Practice paying attention to people when they speak. When you go to the store, become aware of the people around you, and treat the checkout person with loving-kindness by putting away your cell phone and engaging him or her in conversation. As you learn to put thoughts away during your practice, incorporate your practice into every aspect of your life.

Take time during the day for short practice sessions. While you are driving, pull over and take five minutes to meditate. If you're at home or at work, find a quiet, secluded place, set the timer on your phone, and spend a few minutes in practice. Like anything else in life, the more you practice, the better you become.

On the road to wellness (mindfulness), to borrow a phrase from Orthodox Christianity, it is equally important to "stop the poison." Mindfulness practice is holistic. It is important to be mindful of the things you put into your body. Are you treating your body with loving-kindness by feeding it things that lead to good health and well-being, or are you poisoning your body by mindlessly filling yourself with fast foods and additives? Are you listening to music that has a life-giving message or are you filling your mind with negative, lustful, or immorally degrading thoughts? Are you allowing yourself to participate in speaking poorly of others or coarse jesting, or are you choosing life-giving words?

Another way to practice mindfulness is by taking a walk in the woods. Take off your shoes and feel the earth. Become aware of how the grass and leaves feel beneath your feet. The most important part when you are in the forest is to stay in the forest, not letting your mind drift away to another place. Enjoy the songs of the birds and notice the tree frogs chirping, the shrill hum of the cicadas, or the sounds of the crickets. Pay attention to diversity of plant life. You may even be blessed by seeing some wildlife. If it rains, enjoy the sensation of the drops falling on your face. Take it all in, and simply be present.

One of my favorite ways of practicing mindfulness is eating ice cream. If you don't like ice cream, practice with whatever food you enjoy. One of my favorite desserts is chocolate peanut butter ice cream. I can't tell you how many times I have been on my last few bites and realize that I really haven't enjoyed it as much as I could have because I have been mindlessly shoveling it in my mouth while my thoughts were a million miles away. The idea of a life of mindfulness is learning to become fully present and fully alive in every moment. Enjoy every bite—feel the texture on your tongue and rejoice right along with your taste buds—not thinking about the next bite or the one before but the one that is in your mouth. Treat that mouthful of frozen bliss as if it were the last bite of ice cream that will ever exist.

> A new beginning! We must learn to live each day, each hour, yes, each minute as a new beginning, as a unique opportunity to make everything new. Imagine that we could live each moment as a moment pregnant with new life. Imagine that we could live each day as a day full of promises. Imagine that we could walk through the new year always listening to a voice saying to us: "I have a gift for you and can't wait for you to see it!" Imagine.[16]

---

[16] Henri Nouwen, *Here and Now: Living In The Spirit* (New York, NY: The Crossroad Publishing Company, 1994), 16.

—Henri Nouwen, *Here and Now:
Living In The Spirit*

4. Faith

It's almost impossible to pick up a book written in the past five years on the subject of recovery from trauma and not find a mention of mindfulness and yoga. Mindfulness and yoga are proven tools for the healing of trauma, but lasting recovery is unlikely without a holistic approach. You can begin the work of healing your conative processes, nervous system, and body, but if you don't nurture your spirit, you will likely continue in a never-ending cycle of frustration.

The mind must be healed. I am not referring to our physical brain but our consciousness. I am talking about that part of us that gives us life beyond being a biological organism. Albert Einstein said, "The more I study science the more I believe in God." The more I study the complexities of the human mind and nervous system, the more I also stand in awe of God. Each one of us is a creation story—a living miracle with so much more value than any one of us will understand on this side of Heaven. We are so much more than biological organisms. It is by God's breath that we exist—His Spirit-giving life. Every emotion comes from God, and every one of God's motives is sparked by emotion.

Sacred Scripture tells us that "The Lord is good to all, and His compassion is over all that He has made (Psalm 145:9). As discussed in chapter twelve, compassion is not sympathy but something that is shared. What the Word of God is communicating to us is that God shares in our emotions. He is not a bystander sitting on the sidelines.

On the contrary, He is an active participant in our lives—in all His Creation. When we experience joy, He experiences joy. When we hurt, He hurts. The Apostle Paul tells us, "If one member [of the Body of Christ] suffers, all suffer together; if one member is honored, all rejoice together" (1 Corinthians 12:26). We are all joined together as one body by the Spirit of God in Christ.

Don't ever let anybody tell you that your emotions are not important. If you are hurting, your story needs to be heard. When God is angry, hurt, or jealous, He speaks without trepidation. We need to learn to do the same in a healthy way. Emotions can, however, lead us astray if they are unhealthy or misunderstood. This is why it is so important for us to seek a good counselor—someone to help us navigate the minefield of misplaced emotions that can so easily sabotage our recovery efforts.

Consider the emotions of anxiety, fear, and anger. For so many of us these emotions evoke shame and increased anxiety, fear, and anger. It becomes a self-perpetuating cycle of dysfunction.

The antidote to shame, anxiety, fear, and anger is trust. When we trust that God loves us enough to forgive us, shame becomes manageable. When we trust God, anxiety, fear, and anger simply fade away like long-forgotten companions. The problem is that so many of us have tried to walk the Christian life without ever trusting God. The evidence is in the shame, anxiety, and anger that we carry.

How many of us have heard the words, "Well, brother/sister, you just need to have more faith." Perhaps you have heard similar words from your pastor or someone offering prayer. I know all too well that hearing such sentiments can be frustrating. It is not that simple, especially when we have grown up learning not to trust anyone.

How do we develop trust? Trust is built through relationship—by getting to know somebody. Trust is a form of intimacy. We can learn about someone and talk about that person for years and never know who they truly are. How many of us have attended church for years and have a deep respect for God, but our actions prove that we really don't trust Him? That was me, as I recounted in the first chapter of this book. I knew the Bible inside and out and spent years in church, but I never got to know God. I didn't know how to trust.

When my understanding of prayer changed, I began to know God a little better. I still have a long way to go, and I still have issues with trusting Him from time to time, especially when He asks me to let go of something or step outside my comfort zone.

Let's take a look at what Henri Nouwen has to say about prayer in his book, *Hear and Now: Living In The Spirit*.

> Prayer is the discipline of the moment. When we pray, we enter into the presence of God whose name is God-with-us. To pray is to listen attentively to the One who addresses us here and now. When we dare to trust that we are never alone but that God is always with us, then we can gradually detach ourselves from the voices that make us guilty or anxious and thus allow ourselves to dwell in the present moment. This is a very hard challenge because radical trust in God is not obvious. Most of us distrust God. Most of us think of God as a fearful, punitive authority or as an empty, powerless nothing. Jesus' core message was that God is neither a powerless weakling nor a powerful boss, but a lover, whose only desire is to give us what our hearts desire.
>
> To pray is to listen to the voice of love. That is what obedience is all about. The word 'obedience' comes from the Latin word ob-audire,

which means to listen with great attentiveness. Without listening we become 'deaf' to the voice of love. The Latin word for deaf is surdus. To be completely deaf is to be absurdus, yes, absurd. When we no longer pray, no longer listen to the voice of love that speaks to us in the moment, our lives become absurd lives in which we are thrown back and forth between the past and the future.[17]

Hesychasm is a method of prayer practiced as a way of helping to quiet the mind of the cares of this life and to enter into the stillness of the Lord's presence within the heart.[18] The term "hesychast" began to emerge in the fourth-century writings of the Church, which is a term used to describe those who practice this form of prayer.[19] The word "hesychasm" is derived for the word "hesychia," which communicates an attitude of silent rest, stillness, or a quiet openness to God.[20]

Hesychasm describes what became a way of life for a group of esthetic hermits (monks) who settled in the Egyptian desert. They sought the silence of the desert as a way of escaping the noise of a corrupt and sinful world in search of union with our Father in Heaven. These monks are better known as the Desert Fathers (and Mothers). They are considered by many to be the pioneers of Christian monasticism.

Traditionally, hesychasm is said to have developed from Christ's instruction as recorded in Matthew 6:6, "But when you pray, go into your room and shut the door and pray to your Father who is in secret; and your Father who

---

[17] Nouwen, *Here and Now*, 22–23.
[18] Ibid., 73–77.
[19] "Hesychasm," *New World Encyclopedia*, accessed September 24, 2020, https://www.newworldencyclopedia.org/entry/Hesychasm.
[20] *The Philokalia*, Volume Two (Queen Square: London, 1981), 387.

sees in secret will reward you."[21] This form of prayer was developed by repeating small portions of scripture or short prayers, such as "Jesus is Lord" or "The Lord is my Shepherd" (Psalm 23:1) until they carved out a place of residence within the heart. Soon different forms of what we refer to today as "The Jesus Prayer" or "The Prayer of the Heart" began to develop. The Jesus prayer is typically associated with the tradition of our Orthodox brothers and sisters, but it is also practiced by many Catholics and Protestants.

Prayer ropes with knots or with beads are often used but are not a necessary part of the prayer. The ropes are not considered holy or sacred but simply aid in focusing the mind. As one prays, the knots or beads are run through the fingers as a way to help concentration. The prayer is repeated slowly with deliberate focus. A pause is suggested between each short prayer for a moment of reflection.[22]

The idea behind hesychastic prayer is to focus our minds completely on God, which is in sharp contrast to the "non doing" attitude of mindfulness meditation. However, when attempting it, you will encounter some of the same difficulties. Your mind will be pulled toward the cares of this life. The silence of the desert is not the absence of audible sound but a position of the heart. In our noisy and hectic world, it is not practical to require absolute silence to hear God's voice, although it is nice to find a quiet place to be with Him at times.

The key is to be able to hear His still, small voice in the midst of the chaos. Any aesthetic will attest to the fact that silence can be deafening. Learning to silence the noise of your mind is one of our greatest challenges. As

---

[21] "Hesychasm," *New World Encyclopedia*, accessed September 24, 2020, https://www.newworldencyclopedia.org/entry/Hesychasm.
[22] Albert S. Rossi, "Saying The Jesus Prayer," *St. Vladimir's Orthodox Theological Seminary*, accessed September 24, 2020, https://www.svots.edu/saying-jesus-prayer.

believers in Jesus Christ, we are called to free our hearts and minds from the deception of this world and to focus our full attention "on things that are above" (Colossians 3:2).

The heart of the desert (the hesychast) is to become obedient to the Scripture and enter a life of unceasing prayer[23] (1 Thessalonians 5:17). That is, as much as humanly possible, to live a life in full communion with God. As we keep our minds on Christ and set our hearts on Him and Him alone, the Holy Spirit will fill our spirits with the "Oil of Heaven." This comes to us during what the Church often refers to as contemplation. The Oil of Heaven is the Holy Spirit who dwells in the heart of every believer. Contemplation happens when the Holy Spirit speaks to us from our hearts.

The Church has practiced meditation and contemplation for centuries. Though going by different names among different groups, the idea of focusing on God and listening for the voice of Love has remained much the same. I think of meditation and contemplation as the ebb and flow of the tides. Think of meditation as the outgoing tide—when we quiet our hearts and focus completely on God. This can be practiced by using short prayers such as the Jesus Prayer or with words of adoration for our Lord. I often spend my time meditating on the goodness and loving-kindness of God, repeating short utterances such as "You are awesome," "You are holy," or "You are good." This does not have to be vocal; it can also be practiced with mental prayer. Think of contemplation as the incoming tide. This is when God responds.

No conversation about meditation and contemplation would be complete without including St. Teresa of Avila. Her writings—and I would like to think her intercession—has been a lifeline during my recovery. When I be-

---

[23] Nouwen, *Here and Now*, 82-85.

gan my recovery process, her writing touched my heart in a way that it desperately needed. Her passion for our Lord and the subject of prayer swept through my spirit like a contagion.

When St. Teresa discusses contemplation in *The Interior Castle*, she describes it as the prayer of quiet. The reason she refers to contemplation as the prayer of quiet is that this prayer is a time for us to be quiet and listen to God's voice.[24] When we are called into His presence, it is time for us to close our mouths, quiet our minds, and listen to what He is saying—the time for meditation is over. This is when God's presence floods our hearts and minds, and we become captivated by Love.

There is an interlude between the meditation and contemplation that St. Teresa calls the prayer of recollection. She describes this brief, fleeting moment with the following words: "Without any labour of one's own, the temple of which I spoke is reared for the soul in which to pray: the senses and exterior surroundings appear to lose their hold, while the spirit gradually regains its lost sovereignty."[25]

I often refer to this prayer of recollection as the prayer of "un-expectancy." This is the moment when we come to the sudden understanding that God's undivided attention is on us. We experience this in the few moments before contemplation when we are called to forget ourselves and focus every ounce of our attention on what our Lord has to say.

I like to think of the prayer of recollection as the moment when my mind becomes fully cognizant of God's presence. Some refer to it as when the soul pulls itself together or, as St. Teresa describes, "the spirit gradually re-

---

[24] Saint Teresa of Avila, *The Interior Castle* (Magisterium Press, 2015), Kindle locations 53–55.
[25] Ibid., 57.

gains its lost sovereignty."[26] I am trying to describe something that is indescribable.

Imagine being in a room dancing with everything you have within you. You are completely alone. You have not an ounce of thought that anyone could be watching. Then you turn around, and there He is, standing in the doorway looking at you with undivided attention. You stop at the sight of this unexpected Visitor (prayer of recollection) partially at the surprise of His presence but mostly in awe that the God of all Creation would take the time to visit you. Now you drop to your knees in humility, and He walks toward you with outstretched arms and a grin that ignites your heart. There is no need for words—the encounter is sufficient. Now it's time to listen with undivided focus to what He has to say (prayer of quiet).

A concept that may be hard to understand at this point is that when we enter meditation, our purpose or goal is not contemplation. In other words, our goal is not to strive harder and harder until God speaks to us. We should long to hear God's voice, but only in His perfect time. The key to meditation is to become content in meditation.

As I am writing, I can't help but think of lyrics from one of my favorite songs, "Breathing," by the band Lifehouse. The lyrics so well describe the heart of the desert.

> *'Cause I am hanging on every word you say*
> *And even if you don't want to speak tonight*
> *That's alright, alright with me*
> *'Cause I want nothing more*
> *than to sit outside heaven's door*
> *and listen to you breathing*
> *Is where I wanna be*

---

[26] Ibid., 69.

where I wanna be
where I wanna be[27]

    The heart of the desert is to grab hold of Jesus with our hearts and with minds and never let go. To strive in mediation is to frustrate our spirit. Learning to wait patiently for God to speak is how we learn to listen. It is how we learn perfect contentment. At times you may go days, weeks, or even months without hearing Him speak, but the moment you hear His voice, you will know that every minute of meditation was worth the effort.

    Thousands of Christians around the world gather every week in the hope of experiencing God's presence and hearing His voice in contemporary praise and worship services. Scripture verses and/or sentiments of adoration are sung in a repetitive nature, usually accompanied by the sounds of keyboards, drums, and guitars, as those in attendance join in—allowing the lyrics and melody to take resonance in their hearts.

    Jesus assures us in His Word, "For where two or three are gathered in my name, there am I in the midst of them" (Matthew 18:20). Some of my sweetest encounters with our Lord have been during corporate worship. God created us for communion. Some accuse the contemporary worship movement of emotionalism. I whole-heartedly agree. When we experience God's presence, it is emotional. We are experiencing the Author and Creator of our emotions. It is He who is able to heal us and put our emotions in the right order.

---

[27] "Breathing." Track 9 on No Name Face. Dreamworks, 2001. Jason Wade.

Chapter 14

Final Thoughts

> And I believe what I believe is what makes me
> what I am
> I did not make it, no it is making me
> It is the very truth of God and not the invention
> of any man
>
> — Rich Mullins, "Creed"

I hope that you have found encouragement and perhaps even a place to begin the next leg of your journey in the pages of this book. For me, this work has been arduous in many ways while at the same time a labor of love. As I shared in the introduction, I had no idea of the struggles I would face along the way. What I did not share is that I have been consistently surprised by love around many of the unexpected twists and turns.

If you are a victim of the trauma of mental, physical, and/or sexual abuse, please do not ever let anyone minimize what you have experienced. The discussion of childhood sexual abuse is uncomfortable for everyone, something most people avoid at all costs. However, the cost of avoidance could be your health and happiness. I pray that you will find the courage to see a counselor, share your story, and begin down your own path of recovery. Please do not wait until your body starts telling your story with symptoms of illness. I am confident that as you let your heart speak, you will be surprised by the love, joy, and compassion that you so desperately deserve.

If your body is beginning to tell your story, healing is available. I am happy to report that my episodes of dissociation have become all but non-existent, and my dysautonomia symptoms are considerably less severe than they were in 2108. Although I am improving, I still struggle. I am fighting the good fight that millions of other souls around the world who suffer with chronic illness fight every day. Some days are good, and other days are not so good, but every day is a blessing from God.

The good news is that my HRV (heart rate variability) scores have gotten better over the past two years. They are consistently ten to fifteen points higher than when I received my first test at the Mayo Clinic two years ago. I will keep doing what I am doing, and hopefully, I will continue to improve. Doctors are learning more about autonomic nervous system disorders every day.

I may never be completely healed on this side of Heaven, and that's OK. It is enough for me to know why—to understand that I have fought the good fight in the aftermath of trauma and rest secure in the arms of my Creator. As odd as it may sound, I'm happy that I am where I am today on my journey. I don't think I could have become the person I am had I not traveled the road I walked. I would have never wished for the pain and suffering that I have experienced, but I am truly thankful for every chisel mark left by the Master Sculptor. God does not cause any of the traumas that we experience, but He can use the substance of our suffering for good (Genesis 50:20). It is only by His hand that we develop our better qualities.

I would love to live another forty to fifty years or longer if it is in God's design for my life. If He has other plans, I admit I will be a bit disappointed, but I have no doubt that His grace will be more than sufficient. The truth is, I love my life despite all the pain and suffering I have experienced. I have suffered much, but having the opportunity to receive a fraction of God's grace and kindness that I have already experienced has made it worth the ride. I want to have the opportunity to live a life of thankfulness, kind of like a "do-over." How happy are we—created by the God of the "do-over." His mercies are new every morning (Lamentations 3:23).

O felix culpa quae talem et tantum meruit habere redemptorem.

May God bless you and keep you.

The End in Love

W. J. Novack

Author's Notes

Bible Translation

The Scripture references are from the Revised Standard Catholic Edition unless otherwise notated.

Stay Connected

Email: bill@wjnovack.com

Web-address: www.wjnovack.com

Facebook: wjnovack.com

Made in the USA
Monee, IL
13 May 2021